John F Fennelly

Memoirs of a bureaucrat

JOHN F. FENNELLY *Title* # Memoirs
# of a
bureaucrat

A *personal story*
of the
War Production Board

OCTOBER HOUSE 1965
Chicago, Illinois

Contents

*Memoirs
of a
bureaucrat*

Introduction

A full generation has passed since Pearl Harbor. Now, at this late date, I find myself overcome by a previously unsuspected urge to put on paper my personal reminiscences of the War Production Board of World War II. Although these events now seem far away and long ago, I have been induced to undertake this task by a number of considerations. First is the belief that the gigantic achievement of American industry during those fateful years, and the part played by the WPB in this effort, provide a story that should never grow old or stale. Second, I believe that these experiences still afford some important lessons for a succeeding generation. Finally, the very passage of time should give to a present day writer certain advantages. The events of those hectic days tend to fall into better perspective, and the story can be freed from most of the personal prejudices and rancours that loomed so large twenty years ago.

Throughout the war years the War Production Board was a center of seething controversy, caused by unending pressures from without, and by continuous explosions from within. Frequently, during those days, I was almost persuaded that the war was being won, not because of, but in spite of the War Production Board. Now I can see that such an opinion was never wholly justified. There was, to be sure, incessant confusion, amounting almost to chaos, in the leadership of the WPB. Throughout all the successive crises at the top, however, the work of the huge staff, particularly at the level of the industry branches, continued to function with a high degree of efficiency and to render important assistance to American business in the overall battle of production for victory.

Moreover, the task of converting the American economy to an all-out war effort, and then of directing this effort into the most effective channels, was of a magnitude and complexity never before undertaken by any group of men. Despite all the bungling and controversy the job somehow was done. I am now convinced that the War Production Board did play a vital role in the winning of the war, and that the many thousands of dedicated men and women on the WPB staff made important contributions toward this goal.

This story makes no pretense of being an overall history of the War Production Board. The WPB organization was necessarily so huge and complex that no one individual could possibly see the picture in all its detail. In addition, my service on the WPB staff was limited roughly to the first year and a half of America's participation in World War II. Thus, I had no direct part in the many months of active defense planning prior to Pearl Harbor, or in the work of the War Production Board after the summer of 1943.

In spite of these limitations of time and space, I feel there were certain aspects of my experiences which should make possible the telling of an interesting story. Thus, my service covered the formative period of the WPB when basic policy decisions were hammered out in sweat and tears, and when the mature pattern of WPB activity finally emerged. Next, my position as Director of the Program Bureau and Vice-Chairman of the Requirements Committee gave me an unusual vantage point to observe and participate in the evolution of a system of allocations which eventually became the chief instrument of control of the whole economy. Finally, it is my conviction that no objective or adequate account of the development of this system of allocations has as yet been presented to the public.

Being a personal report of one man's experiences, this is more a story of personalities than it is a chronological record of events. For this reason I feel no need to apologize for the constant use of the personal pronoun. Perhaps I should apologize in advance for minor inaccuracies that may have crept into the account after the lapse of twenty years. No man's memory is perfect and I am sure that mine is not. I can only say in this connection that I have been astonished by the wealth of detail that has flowed back into my memory since I began to focus my mind on this subject. I am confident that these recollections are accurate in essential details, although doubtless I have been guilty of minor lapses here and there.

For anyone who was not overcome by the importance of his own role in the war effort, there was a great deal of humor to be found in the life at the WPB. Some of this humor I have attempted to recapture in its original and salty form. I can only hope that my readers will not be offended by the coarseness of some of these stories. To my mind they constitute an essential part of the atmosphere of the period.

The lack of a sense of humor shown by some of my colleagues arose mainly, I am sure, from an excess of zeal for winning the war. Thus, those who came to

Washington in 1941, and even in 1940, to help in the early defense planning carried in themselves the fervor of crusaders. They gave the impression of a determination by their own personal efforts to wipe out the menace of Hitlerism. This group called themselves "all-outers" and tended to look down from Olympian heights on those lesser mortals like myself who only arrived on the scene after the actual outbreak of hostilities.

There can be no doubt as to the sincerity of these zealots and I have no desire to disparage their sense of dedication. I can only point out that this very fervor was a contributing cause of the almost continuous controversies that rent the War Production Board. Frequently these individuals appeared as ready to battle anyone who did not agree with their own theories of waging the war as they were to fight the Nazis and the Japs.

A similar situation prevailed in the military services and in the other civilian agencies. Each official responsible for a given program became convinced that the war would be lost unless he was able to obtain the resources necessary to carry out his own project. As an extreme example of this myopic zeal I remember seeing a representative of the Board of Economic Warfare break down and weep in a crowded room when I was forced to cut back severely the agency's request for strategic materials to be shipped to Latin America.

It was obviously impossible to supply all of the materials, facilities and manpower for all of the planned programs. The task of serving as umpire over these many competing claims was not a happy one, particularly if you were aware of the sincerity with which these claims were pressed. Every claimant had to be disappointed to a greater or lesser degree, and the resulting frustrations and controversies threatened constantly to tear the War Production Board apart.

I cannot emphasize too strongly that there is no intent in these pages to reflect any discredit upon our armed forces. The heroic achievement of our fighting men in the front lines all over the world forms no part of this story. For the members of the services of supply in Washington I felt nothing but sympathy and understanding. Frustrated by being forced to serve so far behind the front lines they were all impelled by an overwhelming desire to provide all possible resources for their brothers who were dying in battle. As a result, they found it very difficult to understand why they could not obtain everything they felt was necessary to carry out their own particular military programs.

Such devotion to the cause was found not only in the military services but also in the wartime civilian agencies. One of the most moving aspects of my service in Washington was an awareness of the high sense of dedication shown in all quarters. Individuals often differed as to the most effective methods for waging the war but there were no laggards in putting their shoulders to the wheel. During the early months of the war most of us worked at least twelve hours a day and frequently seven days a week. To have been a part of this tremendous effort will always be a source of pride for me.

Finally, I offer my apologies to the large number of good friends on the War Production Board staff who are not even mentioned in this book. My story is necessarily so restricted in scope that any effort to introduce the names of those who were not directly connected with the problems discussed herein could only lead to confusion and misunderstanding. The omission of these names does not mean that such individuals did not play important roles in the work of the WPB, but merely that they did not happen to fit directly into the pattern of this particular story.

Personal background

Although this small volume is in no sense an auto-biography, a brief outline of my adult background seems relevant for the purposes of this story. It should serve to explain my attitude toward our country's participation in World War II, and my general frame of mind during my service with the War Production Board.

During the first World War I served for six months as a flying cadet in what was then known as the Army Air Corps—three months in ground school at Berkeley, California, and an almost equal period of flying instruction at March Field, Riverside, California. Except for the frustrating fact that I never saw any battle action, it was for me a lovely war. I was just nineteen, the California skies were bright, the California girls were blonde and beautiful, and I was in the most glamorous of all services.

Looking backward from the Nineteen Sixties, it is not easy to understand the extent to which I idealized the glories of war in 1918. I took to the military as though I had been born to it, and I never learned anything of the horror and tragedy of an actual battlefield. With the perfervid imagination of youth I visualized the career of a military aviator as the quintessence of knighthood in flower, and I was determined to be the "parfait gentil" knight riding forth to slay a dragon.

The only tragedy in my military career was the abrupt ending of the war in November 1918, before my flying training was completed. I felt humiliated and cheated, and believed it would be difficult to face my contemporaries who had had the great good fortune to serve on the battlefields of France. Another complex from which I suffered was the fear that the military distinctions between officers and enlisted men would persist in peace time, and that I would find myself a second-class citizen if I returned to Princeton University without my wings and a second lieutenancy.

As a result, I resisted for almost two months after the Armistice the strenuous efforts of my parents to induce me to resign from the Air Corps and return to college. I finally succumbed to parental pressure early in January 1919, and rejoined my class at Princeton. Of course, I found no social distinctions between my older classmates who had fought in France and the less fortunate youngsters like myself. Consequently, I had an extremely happy time for the next eighteen months and graduated with my class in June of 1920.

During the next decade my viewpoint on the role of the United States in World War I and on war in general turned full cycle. Viewing the tragedies and convulsions of postwar Europe I could no longer believe that our country had done anything to make the world safe for democracy. I even reached the conclusion that a more lasting and satisfactory peace in Europe would probably have been accomplished if we had not intervened.

7

This change in outlook was largely the result of my scholarly activities during my early postgraduate years. Prior to the summer of 1929, when I entered the investment banking business, I had engaged in a varied and hectic assortment of pursuits. After a brief tour as a reporter on the Kansas City Star, I taught history for a year at the Country Day School of Kansas City. I then spent two years in my father's grain business in Kansas City and St. Louis. Leaving this at the end of 1923, I returned to Princeton and acquired a doctorate of philosophy in economics in 1927. Finally, I served for two years as an instructor in economics and history at Columbia University.

Memoirs
of a
bureaucrat

Thus, as the war clouds began to gather in Europe and Asia in the Thirties, I found myself a firm believer in a role of strict neutrality for the United States. These

The author,
shortly after the end
of World War II

convictions became even stronger after the outbreak of war in Europe in 1939. During the next two years, the steady drift of the United States toward intervention, and the pressures exerted by the Roosevelt administration in this direction were obvious to the most casual observer.

I resented particularly what I regarded as President Roosevelt's insincerity in leading our country step by step down the road to war while promising at the same time to keep us out of it. It is possible that this resentment made me underestimate the menace of the Nazis and the Japanese. Nevertheless, nothing has happened during the intervening years to cause me to admit that such was the case. Beneath the level of my surface irritation I had developed a set of convictions that seemed then, and still seem sound and logical.

First, I regarded it as almost inevitable that our intervention would involve us and western Europe in a series of tragic mistakes similar to those that had followed in the wake of World War I. We would have to bet on Great Britain's ability to provide leadership for postwar Europe and I could see very little hope in this connection. In fact, I was convinced that Britain's day as a world power had passed, and that she would prove as incapable of playing a constructive role in future European affairs as France had been after the end of World War I.

Second, it seemed clear to me that all of the small national states of western Europe had become anachronisms in the world of the Twentieth Century. Faced with the competition of huge continental empires such as the United States and Russia, there was no doubt in my mind that these little principalities must either unite or perish. Thus, the creation of a United States of western Europe had become a fetich in my thinking. I was sure that this development would have to be worked out by the constituent nations themselves, and that intervention by the United States could only retard progress in this direction.

Finally, I was convinced that the real enemy of the United States was International Communism as personified by Soviet Russia. In comparison, the threats of Nazi Germany and Imperial Japan seemed to me relatively minor in importance. Moreover, I had developed a strong admiration for the virility of both the German and Japanese peoples. In fact, I felt that in a final showdown with communism these two nations might prove to be the only strong allies on whom the United States could depend. I never entertained the slightest doubt that, if the United States should enter the war, the certain outcome would be the total destruction of both Germany and Japan. Feeling as I did, however, about the importance of these countries to a future free world, I could not be happy over the prospect.

My views on this whole subject were set forth in detail in a letter that I wrote in December, 1940. It was addressed to my friend, Herbert Agar, then editor of the Louisville Courier-Journal, and was written in reply to a particularly bellicose editorial which Agar had just published. The letter is presented as an appendix at the end of this volume. I hope it will provide interesting reading for those who, at the time, regarded all non-interventionists as members of the lunatic fringe, or even something considerably less attractive.

Despite these strong convictions, I knew my conscience would never permit me to remain on the sidelines if and when my country became involved in a global war. At the age of 42, and without any military training since 1918, I realized that any direct contribution I might make to the armed forces would necessarily

11

be minor. On the other hand, I believed that my training as an economist and banker could prove of value in some civilian role in the war effort. As a result, I set myself firmly against the idea of ever becoming an armchair officer, and began to explore the possibilities of a civilian job in government. This decision led me into the War Production Board in Washington, and it was one I never had any cause to regret.

As a semi-rational preparation for the big event I spent a large part of 1941 in helping to write a book under the auspices of the National Bureau of Economic Research. The three co-authors were W. L. Crum, professor of economics at Harvard, Lawrence H. Seltzer, professor of economics at Wayne University in Detroit, and myself. The original title selected for the volume was "Fiscal Planning for Defense". The manuscript was completed and approved for publication on the eve of Pearl Harbor. As a result of this catastrophic development the authors were forced into a frantic revision of the manuscript. The book was finally published in the spring of 1942 with the title—"Fiscal Planning for Total War".

A
footnote
on
Pearl Harbor

Ever since the event, the mystery of our military disaster at Pearl Harbor has intrigued me. I have read practically all of the important literature on the subject but have yet to read a satisfactory explanation for the total surprise achieved by the Japanese. I am familiar with the widely held theory that Franklin Roosevelt deliberately planned the cataclysm as the only certain means of involving the United States in the War. As a strong opponent of Roosevelt, and of much that he stood for, it might have seemed easy for me to have been able to accept such a theory. Nevertheless, I have always felt that this viewpoint is extremely naive, and accords to our wartime President a degree of Machiavellian cunning which I am sure he did not possess. To me the real explanation is much more simple, but it is one I have never seen set forth in print.

During this period I was fortunate in having a somewhat unusual source of confidential information in Washington. This source was the late Norman H. Davis, who was my father-in-law. Under-Secretary of State in the Woodrow Wilson administration and Ambassador-at-Large in the early Roosevelt years, Mr. Davis served during the War until his death as Chairman of the American Red Cross. He was also one of the closest friends and probably the most confidential advisor of the Secretary of State, Cordell Hull.

During the fall of 1941 I had occasion to make several brief visits to Washington. On a Monday night early in November, I found myself staying at the Davis home in Alexandria, Virginia. It was, I remember, the day before local elections were scheduled to take place in New York, when the New York Stock Exchange would be closed. Mrs. Davis was away and Mr. Davis and I were dining alone.

Halfway through the meal Mr. Davis was called to the phone and was gone for a long time. When he returned his face was grim, but he remarked in a casual tone:

"That was Cordell. He tells me that, as a result of the breaking of the Japanese code, he has learned that some dramatic development in our relations with Japan is scheduled to take place within the next twenty-four hours. He has yet no idea what it may be, but is afraid it might even be a declaration of war."

The next morning at breakfast Mr. Davis was called again to the phone. This time he came back with a broad grin on his face and said:

"Cordell again. He tells me he now understands the new development will be an announcement by the Japanese of the appointment of a special envoy by the name of Kurusu who will come to Washington in a final effort to reach an understanding with our government."

The news of the Kurusu appointment appeared in the papers on the following morning.

This was my first knowledge of the breaking of the Japanese code and of the extraordinary wealth of detailed information regarding the Japanese which became available to our top officials in Washington. How then, with all this knowledge, could the tragedy of Pearl Harbor have occurred as a complete surprise?

A simple answer was suggested to me by Mr. Davis in January of 1942 shortly after my move to Washington. It was implicit in a dialogue which Mr. Davis had with Frank Knox, Secretary of the Navy, on the Saturday morning before Pearl Harbor. About ten-thirty that morning Knox called Davis and invited him to play golf at the Burning Tree Golf Club. After the Secretary's limousine had picked up Mr. Davis at the Red Cross headquarters the following exchange took place between the two men:

Norman Davis—"Frank, I am amazed that you are able to get away and play golf today. Aren't you as certain as I am that the Japs are planning to attack this weekend? Aren't you also concerned about a possible attack on Pearl Harbor?"

Frank Knox—"Don't give it a thought, Norman. Sure, we know the Japs are planning to attack this weekend, but we also know exactly what they are going to do. They will move straight south down the Malayan coast, and there is not the remotest possibility of a strike at Pearl Harbor."

Ever since then it has seemed clear to me that the real villain of the piece was the breaking of the Japanese code and the resulting cocksureness this development

15

gave to our top officials. They became so certain that they knew every detail of Japanese plans that they ruled out the possibility of any surprise. This frame of mind accounts for the instructions to the Hawaiian command for an alert against sabotage rather than a full scale military alert. It also accounts for the long horseback ride in Rock Creek Park taken by General Marshall on the fateful Sunday morning. Our military authorities were so confident in the knowledge available to them that they were even lulled into overlooking the cessation of intercepts from the Japanese carrier fleet which disappeared into radio silence about ten days before Pearl Harbor.

Thus, it is my conviction that, if we had failed to break the code, the possibility of our being caught flatfooted would have been greatly reduced. Our military were fully aware of the importance of the element of surprise in the history of Japanese warfare. In the absence of any special information they would have been forced to be alert to any possible contingencies. To my mind it was a classic example of the old bromide about the danger of a limited amount of knowledge.

16

Early days
in
Washington

O n January 16, 1942, I was still working at my desk
in Chicago as a partner of the investment banking firm
of Glore, Forgan & Co. On that date I received the call I
had been hoping for. It came from Jim Knowlson in
Washington. Knowlson, the president of Stewart-Warner Corporation, had gone to Washington some months
earlier to take a leading role in the Office of Production
Management. His telephone call was to urge me to
come to Washington as promptly as possible and to
serve as his assistant in the War Production Board
which had just been established.

Since this was exactly the kind of opportunity for
which my background and experience seemed best suited, I wasted little time in making up my mind. Within a

week I had closed up my business affairs, resigned as a partner of my firm, and departed for Washington, leaving my family behind to follow later when I had been able to find a home for them.

I wish to emphasize the fact that I resigned from my firm. I took this action deliberately although I realized it would mean supporting my wife and three children on a government salary which would be only a small fraction of what I had been earning in the investment business. I was also fully aware that the great majority of business executives, who were serving their country in the war effort, were doing so under what was known as "the dollar a year" plan. Under this arrangement they were paid only this token annual compensation by the government, but were allowed to retain the full salaries paid to them by their respective businesses. I rejected this idea for a number of reasons.

First, I was not sure what I might wish to do at the end of the war, and I was determined not to be under obligation to my partners as a result of permitting them to support me during my wartime service. Second, I was afraid there could be embarrassing conflicts of interests between my business associations and my work in the War Production Board. Finally, I was concerned about the potential conflict between the permanent civil servants working on small salaries, and the business executives who were able to retain their normal high standards of living. I shall return to the impact of this last point later in this story.

On the same day that I received my telephone call from Knowlson, the press reported the creation of the War Production Board. Prior to this event, economic mobilization had been under the direction of the OPM, or Office of Production Management. This governmental authority, which was established in January, 1941, had limited powers to grant priorities for defense production. It functioned under the combined leadership of William Knudsen, the Danish-born president of General Motors, and Sidney Hillman, prominent labor union official.

As the months of 1941 slipped by, the volume of military orders flowing to American factories reached very large proportions. These orders, piled on top of unrestricted civilian demand, had created, by the summer of 1941, an alarming log jam in the flow of goods and materials, and a progressive depreciation in the currency value of priorities.

A priority order gave to a procuring agency the right to have its desired end products placed in the production schedule of a manufacturer ahead of orders that carried lower priority ratings or no priorities at all. This scheme worked satisfactorily as long as priority rated orders remained moderate in relation to manufacturing capacities. The basic trouble, however, was that no effort at this time had been made to limit the issuance of priorities to plant and material capacities. Instead, as log jams developed, the only solution found was to grant progressively higher priority ratings on new orders. This, of course, moved the old priority rated orders back on the production schedules, reduced their value as priorities and created greater confusion than ever.

In an effort to bring some order out of the developing chaos, a new organization was created on August 28, 1941. This was designated as the Supplies, Priorities and Allocations Board, popularly known as SPAB. Donald M. Nelson, a vice-president of Sears, Roebuck and Co., and formerly Director of Purchases in OPM, was named executive director of SPAB.

This new board, which had no general powers of control over the whole economy, struggled during the fall of that year to reclassify outstanding priority orders and to control the issuance of new priorities. It also succeeded in placing under direct allocation certain critical materials, such as steel plates and aluminum sheets. All of these efforts, however, represented piecemeal attacks on the problem and never came to grips with the growing need for establishing complete control over the whole economy.

After the outbreak of global warfare in December of 1941, the necessity of creating a comprehensive system of controls over the national economy could no longer be ignored. The result was the birth of the War Production Board in January, 1942, established under the wartime powers of the President. The WPB immediately absorbed the large organization of OPM and the smaller organization of SPAB.

Donald Nelson was named chairman of the WPB and was vested with almost dictatorial powers over the American economy. Although members of the board included the Vice-President, the Secretary of War, the Secretary of the Navy, the Secretary of Commerce, the

*Donald M. Nelson, Chairman
of the War Production Board,
1942-1944*

head of the Office of Price Administration, and top military officials, the board as such had no authority other than to act as advisors to the Chairman.

Donald Nelson was, prior to Pearl Harbor and for at least a year thereafter, a darling of the New Dealers. I first met Nelson in 1939 in Washington. He was introduced to me by a government official as "the greatest living American industrialist". This opinion, I may add, was not shared by Nelson's former associates in Sears, Roebuck, who considered him primarily a politician and only secondarily a businessman.

As a result of almost two years of close observation of Nelson, I found myself in hearty agreement with the opinion of the Sears, Roebuck management. In my judgment, he never showed qualities of courageous leadership, he was a poor administrator, and was at all times under the domination of the White House palace guard.

One result of the January shuffle was the elimination of Bill Knudsen, who had served as head of OPM. As president of General Motors, Knudsen, was of course, no favorite of the New Dealers. As a face-saving device, Roosevelt made Knudsen a lieutenant-general in the Army in charge of expediting war production in the field. It is my understanding that in this capacity Knudsen performed a magnificent service for the nation.

When I reported for duty at Jim Knowlson's office, I found the War Production Board ensconced in the Social Security Building and filling every nook and cranny of this huge structure. Knowlson at this time had the position of Director of Industry Production. As such he was second in command to the chairman, Donald Nelson. I was given a desk in the office of Blackwell Smith, another assistant to Jim Knowlson. My tiny desk, which I occupied for the next two months, was behind the door of the office and pushed up flush against a blank wall.

Blackie Smith, whose destiny and mine were closely linked during the next nine months, was a handsome, dark-haired lawyer of about my age. He was crammed equally with energy and ideas, but suffered from the handicap of expressing his opinions in the most complicated verbiage I have ever heard from the mouth of an otherwise intelligent man. There was a classic story told of a discussion between Smith and Bill Knudsen in the early days of the OPM. After listening to Blackie expound an idea for about ten minutes, Knudsen broke in with: "Dumb it down, Blackie, Dumb it down! I haven't understood a word you have said."

At first the War Production Board seemed to me nothing more than a booming confusion. In those early days no one appeared to be considering the possibility of a comprehensive and integrated plan for controlling the national economy. Instead, everyone was dashing around frantically in an effort to break specific bottlenecks in production or to expedite the flow of badly needed military items.

My early assignments were all of this trouble shooting character. Actually much of this work involved a cutting back of military orders for civilian types of equipment. With the outbreak of hostilities each separate military procurement agency had piled orders for civilian type goods into our manufacturing establishments. This was done without regard for their own overall needs, without regard to basic civilian requirements, and with no thought whatsoever to the necessity of converting most of these plants to the production of actual munitions of war.

Thus, my first job was an effort to pry loose some Diesel locomotives for the hard pressed railroads. This brought me into my first head-on collision with the Navy. I quickly discovered that naval officials had pre-empted the entire Diesel engine manufacturing capacity of the country and were extremely loath to admit the validity of any other claims but their own. After a couple of weeks of bickering and negotiation I achieved some measure of success. Arrangements were made to permit a steady though moderate flow of Diesel locomotives for the railroads.

Next, the problem of typewriter production was thrown into my lap. Military officials were starting to scream their heads off over the failure of the War Production Board to convert the typewriter industry to direct military production, and the matter threatened to become a cause célèbre. I soon discovered, however, that orders for typewriters by military agencies were sufficient to operate the entire industry at capacity for more than three years. The Army alone had placed orders for more than one million machines, or approximately one for every three individuals in that service. When I brought this matter to the attention of the Army officials, I asked them if they intended to fight the war with typewriters, and which they would prefer to use against the Germans and Japs—machine guns or typewriters.

The result was an immediate squelching of the incipient explosion. Orders were promptly entered restricting all military orders for new typewriters to a total of 250,000 units and the restriction of civilian purchases entirely to second-hand machines. From that point on the conversion of this important industry proceeded rapidly.

These early successes induced Jim Knowlson to appoint me as chairman of a new committee which he designated as "The End Products Committee". Its task was to inquire into the status of each important segment of civilian type hardware. The objective was to rationalize to the extent possible both military and civilian orders. The anticipated result was both a saving of strategic materials, chiefly metals, and the conversion of additional plant capacity to direct military production.

Since this committee proved to be the prototype of the later full-blown Requirements Committee, it seems desirable to discuss its organization in some detail. Membership on the committee consisted of representatives of the principal claimant agencies—the Army, the Navy, the Air Force, the Maritime Commission, the Lend-Lease Administration, the office of Civilian Supply, and the Bureau of Economic Warfare which handled the requirements of Latin America. In addition to myself as chairman, we had a vice-chairman and a secretary to keep a permanent record of the proceedings. The first vice-chairman was Ernest Quantrell, a retired investment banker from Chicago. The first secretary was Frederick Roe, also from Chicago, who later became head of one of the leading investment counsel firms of the country.

Authority to make decisions was vested in me as chairman, subject to the right of appeal to the chairman of the War Production Board on the part of any dissatisfied agency. Only once during the life of the committee was such an appeal taken. This was the result of the Navy's refusal to accept my decision prohibiting them from ordering new electric fans for use in their shore establishments. The obvious necessity for electric fans in the bowels of ships was recognized by everyone. I am pleased to report that Don Nelson supported me in turning down the appeal.

Once the formation of the committee was announced, many of the other agencies attempted to obtain representation. All of these requests were refused with the exception of the Office of War Transportation, a representative of which was soon added.

An interesting experience occurred in connection with the surprising request of the Canadian Government for membership on the committee. Mr. Carswell, Canadian Deputy Minister of Supply in Washington, first appealed to Jim Knowlson who referred him to me. When Jock Carswell entered my office I was suffering from a bad sinus infection and must have been in a particularly unpleasant humor.

I first told Carswell it would be impossible to grant his request because the whole theory of the committee was that it should include only agencies of the United

James S. Knowlson, Program Vice-Chairman
of the War Production Board, 1942,
and Vice-Chairman of
the Combined Production and Resources Board,
in a photograph taken just before
the beginning of World War II

States Government. I then added the following gratuitous comments:

"You know, Mr. Carswell, it would help us all a lot if the Canadian Government would decide through what American agency it wished to funnel its requirements instead of scattering its requests all over the landscape. The trouble is you give us the impression on Mondays that you are a member of the British Commonwealth of Nations; on Tuesdays that you are a free, independent republic; and on Wednesdays that you are nothing less than the 49th State of the United States."

These remarks ended the interview. The only important footnote is the fact that Jock Carswell and I later became fast friends. One of the most delightful of my wartime experiences was a visit to Canada to inspect some Canadian war plants and to study Canadian methods of allocating strategic materials. This visit was made under the aegis of Jock Carswell and proved to be a thoroughly interesting and pleasant excursion.

During the spring and early summer of 1942 the End Products Committee surveyed a wide range of civilian products. These included all types of office machinery, metal furniture, safes, electric fans, refrigerators, washing machines, radios, etc. In many cases we were astonished to discover the huge amounts of such articles the armed services had on order. Restraining orders of varying degrees of severity were entered which limited both military and civilian use of these types of hardware. The net effect was a substantial saving of strategic materials, and the freeing up of important plant capacity for direct military production.

Another aspect of war production with which I became involved during this period was the problem of financing the conversion of civilian plants to a wartime footing. Early in 1942 the military became alarmed over the absence of any adequate financing vehicle to enable manufacturers to make this drastic shift. Heat was put on Jim Knowlson to find a solution of this problem. Jim in turn called in his old friend, Mark Brown, who was at that time executive vice-president of the Harris Trust and Savings Bank of Chicago. Mark Brown, a Hoosier from Kokomo, Indiana, was brought to Chicago by A. W. Harris and soon made a name for himself as one of the leading commercial bankers of the Middle West. Short and stout, Brown's language was always salty and refreshingly to the point. He wore pince-nez glasses attached to a cord. Whenever he wished to drive home a conclusion he would remove these glasses and wave them in front of his listener like a baton in the hand of an orchestra leader.

Mark Brown came immediately to Washington and I was asked by Knowlson to accompany Mark to a special meeting on the problems of financing in the old War Department building. Arriving at our destination, we found ourselves with a group of grim-faced Army officers seated around a table.

Almost immediately a young major opened the attack. He cited the case of a small manufacturer who had been unable to find financing through any of the normal channels for the conversion of his factory to munitions production. Finishing his story the major shook his finger at Mark and said:

"Mr. Brown, this is no isolated instance. I tell you there are ten thousand cases like this throughout the United States and it is a damned outrage."

Carefully removing his pince-nez, Mark looked the major squarely in the eye and replied:

"Major, in the first World War, if an officer had spoken to me like that, I would have said, 'Yes Sir', and I would have wet my pants. Now I am fifty-four years

29

old, I am in civilian clothes, and I tell you what you say is a lot of God-damned nonsense. There are not ten thousand cases like that in the United States; there are not even ten."

Having completely deflated the young major, Brown went to work seriously on the drafting of a regulation to provide for the necessities of wartime industrial financing. The result was the creation of the V-loan, under which the Federal Government could guarantee up to 95 percent of any bank loan granted for the purpose of facilitating war production.

Thunder
on the left

During February and March of 1942 we all became aware of a gathering storm cloud in Washington over the functioning of the War Production Board under business leadership. The storm was brewed primarily by members of the New Deal bureaucracy both within and without the WPB, and secondarily by the Armed Services who were impatient for all-out munitions production. Prominent amongst the New Dealers who led the attack were Vice-President Wallace, and Leon Henderson, head of the Office of Price Administration. The charge was that the WPB officials were too tender with business, and laggard in forcing the conversion of civilian factories. The chief targets of the attack were Jim Knowlson, Director of Industry Production, and Philip

D. Reed, who was in charge of all the Industry Branches of the WPB. Phil Reed was at that time the very able and attractive chairman of the General Electric Corporation.

The crisis was brought to a head in March by a member of the WPB staff named Robert Guthrie. At the time Guthrie was serving as head of the Textile Branch which was certainly pretty far removed from the problem of direct military production. In any event, Guthrie suddenly resigned his post and called a press conference to give publicity to the reasons for his action. He stated that his resignation was offered as a protest against the failure of the War Production Board leadership to convert American business to military production with sufficient speed.

I became aware of the seriousness of the situation when Knowlson called me into his office on Good Friday. He advised me he had been ordered to make a defense of his policies before a full-dress meeting of the War Production Board the following Tuesday afternoon. He then gave me the assignment of drafting a statement for him to read.

Considerably taken aback, I inquired: "What am I supposed to say?"

Jim's answer was typical of him: "Oh, hell—you know my policies as well as I do. Just set them forth in the kind of clear English you are capable of writing."

With this meager instruction I spent the entire Easter weekend writing and rewriting a statement for Knowlson to deliver. I cited the case of the typewriter industry where we had found plant capacities overwhelmed by orders from the military. I cited other industries which were not scheduled to receive the machine tools necessary for munitions production until the late summer of 1942. If such industries were forced to terminate all civilian production several months earlier, the one certain result would be the loss of practically all of their skilled workmen. I closed by pointing out that the time schedule for the conversion of each industrial plant had to be judged separately, and on its own merits, and that nothing but chaos would result from the sudden stoppage of all civilian production on some arbitrary date.

When I presented the draft to Knowlson on the Monday morning after Easter, he expressed himself as pleased with it and made only a few minor suggestions of changes. The following exchange then took place:

Myself—"Jim, you know I have never seen the august War Production Board in session. Would you mind if I came to the meeting with you and sat in your corner and waved a towel?"

Knowlson—"You don't think for one minute that I am worried about this situation. Well, come along anyway; it won't do you any harm."

The following afternoon I went with Knowlson to the War Production Board meeting. The Board was gathered around a table in a huge, barn-like room. I recognized the Vice-President, the Secretary of War, the Secretary of the Navy, the Secretary of Commerce, Leon Henderson, General Somervell, Admiral Robinson, and Donald Nelson. Finding a chair in a remote corner I tried to make myself as invisible as possible.

Seating himself next to Nelson, Jim Knowlson began reading the statement. The effect of hearing my own words from another's mouth gave me a panicky feeling. They sounded stilted and pompous, and I was certain would cause the downfall of my boss and sponsor.

When Knowlson finished the reading, Don Nelson picked up the cudgels for him.

"As an illustration of the problems Mr. Knowlson has been discussing, I should like to cite the case of the pin-

33

ball game manufacturers. Certainly no one could justify the production of pin-ball games as essential to the war effort. The facts are, however, that these plants possess substantial reservoirs of skilled workmen, and they are not scheduled to receive their new machine tools for war production until June and July. If now we should cut off all production of pin-ball games, these factories would be certain to lose the great bulk of their working forces before their new machine tools can be installed."

At this point, to the surprise of everyone, the whiny, nasal twang of Henry Wallace broke into the discussion:

"You know, Don, I don't see why everyone gets so upset about pin-ball games. They don't do any harm; they provide a lot of innocent amusement; and they do mop up a great deal of excess purchasing power."

This apparent capitulation to the ranks of the enemy on the part of his peerless leader was too much for Leon Henderson to stand. His rasping voice exploded:

"Hell, Henry, if you're concerned about the mopping up of excess purchasing power, I have a much better scheme than pin-ball games. Let's establish a coast-to-coast string of Cat Houses. We will charge $100 per head, and we'll mop up more purchasing power than you can imagine without the use of any scarce materials whatsoever."

During the ensuing outburst of laughter, it became apparent that the uprising against Knowlson had collapsed, and that he was safe for the time being at least. Nevertheless, the New Deal gang was still determined to have its pound of flesh, and succeeded in making Phil Reed the sacrificial lamb of the attack.

To the New Dealers, Reed, as chairman of General Electric, was the archetype of big business executive, and they were determined to eliminate him from the

War Production Board. I never heard of any specific charges made against Phil Reed, and I doubt very much that there were any. Nevertheless, the pressure was such that Reed resigned from the WPB staff in the spring of 1942. During the balance of the war years he performed outstanding service as deputy to Averill Harriman in the London Office of the Lend-Lease Administration.

The evolution of the Requirements Committee

Chapter v i

I

The Production Requirements Plan

By the spring of 1942 growing alarm was evident in the War Production Board and in the Armed Services over the lack of any coordinated plan of control for the entire economy. Even prior to Pearl Harbor the need had been recognized for a central authority with full powers to divide up the national output in a manner which would provide the most efficient flow of materials and products for an all-out war effort.

Thus, during the fall of 1941, a Requirements Committee (a nomenclature adopted from the British system of making allocations) was established within the framework of the Supplies, Priorities, and Allocations Board. Since SPAB, however, had limited powers of control, the efforts of this committee were restricted largely to a reclassification of outstanding priorities and the allocation of a few critical items such as steel plates and aluminum sheets.

Within a few days after the creation of the War Production Board in January 1942, Nelson established a new Requirements Committee within the WPB. William L. Batt, director of the WPB Materials Division, was appointed chairman. Membership on the committee consisted of representatives of the principal agencies which were the chief claimants for scarce materials—the Army, the Navy, the Board of Economic Warfare, the Lend-Lease Administration, the Maritime Commission, and the Division of Civilian Supply.

Unfortunately, this original Requirements Committee of the WPB proved little more effective than its predecessor under SPAB. It had no clearly defined area of authority and no agreed-upon system within which to establish overall controls. Aside from the allocation of a few critical items, the committee was forced to spend most of the first five months of 1942 in discussions and arguments as to how best to establish such controls. As a representative of Jim Knowlson, I sat in on several of these meetings and was forced to report that the discussions generated more heat than light. There was no dispute as to need for a plan of centralized controls but there was no semblance of any agreement as to the best method for putting such a plan into effect. At least a half dozen different plans were discussed, and each had its own group of supporters, both within and outside of the WPB.

Because of the long delay in establishing an overall system of allocations, the national economy, for more than a year after Pearl Harbor, was controlled and converted to war production largely by various types of priority regulations and by a host of separate restraining and limitation orders. Thus, all passenger automobile production was terminated on February 1, 1942. Many other industries were severely limited in their production of civilian goods as a result of actions such as those taken by the End Products Committee and similar actions taken in many other sectors of the economy.

For a while this shotgun method seemed to work reasonably well. Its inadequacies began to appear, however, when the volume of wartime demands mounted to levels that threatened to overwhelm the industrial capacity of the nation. Thus, it soon became apparent that a priority order provided no assurance that the agency to whom it had been issued would be able to obtain the desired goods. Instead a priority became little more than a hunting license with which the military agencies might or might not be successful in obtaining what they needed. A basic trouble was that these priorities were issued by separate agencies without any effort to coordinate them at the top or to limit the total issued to the overall industrial capacity of the economy. The situation led to steadily increasing confusion and a growing sense of frustration on the part of the military authorities.

As a result, a steadily rising demand developed for a system of definite allocations under which the total industrial capacity would be divided equitably amongst the several military agencies and the essential needs of the civilian sector of the economy. Of fundamental importance, of course, was the necessity of limiting total allocations to total industrial capacity so that each agency would be assured of obtaining the products for which it had been granted allocations.

The United States had never before in its history been confronted with an economic problem of such magnitude and complexity. Military production in World War I had been on a much smaller scale and the solutions found at that time were considerably easier to accomplish. Eventually the problem in World War II was solved by what in retrospect appears to have been a very simple and straightforward technique. In the interim, however, the difficulties in the way of a solution seemed vast and practically insurmountable. The result was that many months elapsed, and one abortive start was made, before a satisfactory answer was found.

The controversy in the spring of 1942 as to the best system of allocations to be established centered largely around the question of whether to use a "vertical" or a "horizontal" method of making allocations. All of the several plans under consideration represented variations of these two basic approaches to the problem. In the vertical method one would start with the end products of the various programs (i.e., the tanks, guns, warships, etc., desired by the military). The amount of basic materials required to complete these programs would then be computed. Finally, within the limits of our national capacity, allocations of such materials would be made to the several claimant agencies to produce the approved programs.

In the horizontal approach, the WPB would make separate allocations of materials to each factory involved in the war effort in accordance with statements of requirements from such plants of the materials needed to complete the orders on their books of end products which carried a given level of priority rating.

From the outset it was clear that the military agencies

favored the vertical approach to allocations. It was natural for them to think in terms of the end products of their tools of trade—so many guns, so many tanks, etc. They also felt that the vertical method would provide the only means of maintaining a tight control over their production schedules. In other words, the allocations would be tied directly to definite military programs which could then be scheduled for completion with a high degree of precision.

In the War Production Board, on the other hand, there was a definite bias in favor of the horizontal approach. First, this method would be more nearly in accord with established procedures. Actually, allocations to separate factories of their total requirements of materials were already being made on a voluntary basis. Thus, it was argued that such a system could be made compulsory for all concerned with a minimum of trouble and within the shortest possible period of time.

It was also believed, with some reason, that separate allocations to individual plants would enable the WPB to maintain a tighter control over the problem of excess inventories. Finally, and particularly amongst New Deal elements, there was a fear that adoption of a vertical system of allocations would transfer from civilian hands to the military a large measure of control over the whole economy. Conversely, it was believed that the horizontal approach would maintain control of the economy in the hands of the War Production Board.

After an almost endless series of arguments and discussions, a decision was finally reached in favor of the horizontal approach. On June 10, 1942, the War Production Board issued General Priority Order No. 10. This directive made compulsory for every plant with war orders in excess of $5,000 the use of the Production Requirements Plan, generally known as PRP. Under this plan, which was already in voluntary use, each factory was required to furnish to the WPB a statement of its actual consumption of twelve different materials, used in the production of 200 different products, for the preceding calendar quarter. It would also furnish a statement of its inventories on hand, and its requirements for the same materials for the ensuing calendar quarter. These requirements were to be broken down in accordance with the different priority ratings of the orders on the factory's books.

The theory was that all of these stated requirements were to be gathered together at the WPB, and the total demand for materials calculated by the process of simple addition. This total demand would then be compared with the anticipated supply of such materials for the same calendar quarter. To the extent that the demand exceeded the supply, a balance would be achieved by the elimination of all orders with relatively low priority ratings. For example, if a balance could only be achieved by allocations for all orders with a priority rating of A-1 or higher, all lower rated orders would have to fall by the wayside.

Concurrently with the issuance of General Priority Order No. 10, Jim Knowlson was appointed Program Vice-Chairman of the War Production Board and Chairman of the Requirements Committee in place of William L. Batt. Knowlson in turn named me Vice-Chairman of the Requirements Committee and chairman of the newly created Program Adjustment Committee, which was to be the working sub-committee of the Requirements Committee. From that moment on I found myself catapulted right into the middle of the Chinese puzzle of making overall allocations.

The relationship between the Requirements Committee and the Program Adjustment Committee was very close. In practically every instance, a top official of each agency was appointed as member of the Requirements Committee and his immediate deputy was made a member of the PAC. Thus, General Lucius Clay, second to General Sommervell in command of the Army Service Forces, became a member of the Requirements Committee, while his deputy, Colonel James Boyd, was the Army's representative on the PAC. Likewise, Admiral Williams represented the Navy on the top committee and his deputy, Captain John Small, served on the PAC.

As the system worked itself out, all the preliminary and detailed work in making allocations was done at the level of the Program Adjustment Committee. Consequently, many of the members of the top committee found it desirable to be in regular attendance at meetings of the PAC. Such was the case with General Clay and Admiral Williams. For the Air Force, Brigadier

General Lucius D. Clay, Commander-in-Chief of the United States Forces in Europe and Military Governor of the U.S. Zone of Occupied Germany, shortly after his appointment as a Four Star General

General Frederick Hopkins was in regular attendance at both committees. An exception to this rule was afforded by the Office of Civilian Supply. The head of this agency, Joseph Weiner, restricted his attendance to the infrequent meetings of the Requirements Committee, while his deputy, Maurice Wertheim, attended regularly the meetings of the PAC.

The first Vice-Chairman of the Program Adjustment Committee was William Black, a partner of the auditing firm of Peat, Marwick & Mitchell. Bill Black, a black Scot, was one of the ablest men I met in Washington and a wonderful associate. Unfortunately for me, Black was persuaded around the end of 1942 to leave Washington and to join the Lend-Lease administration in London. His place in turn was taken by Charles Kohlhepp, a utility executive from Milwaukee. Charlie Kohlhepp succeeded me as chairman of the Program Adjustment Committee when I resigned in June of 1943.

Fred Roe, the former secretary of the End Products Committee, moved up to become secretary of the Requirements Committee. Charles Capek, of the Lee Higginson Corporation, was made Secretary of the PAC.

The original directive of June 10 made PRP compulsory for the third quarter of 1942. Almost immediately, however, everyone realized that the time allotted for the gathering and compiling of requirements, and the making of allocations was ridiculously short. As a result, the deadline for making PRP effective was quickly shifted to the last quarter of the year. Even so, the three additional months of grace proved insufficient for the task involved.

The paper work imposed by the plan on each of the thousands of separate factories throughout the nation was immense. The job of compiling requirements for each of a long list of materials, and then of breaking these requirements down into separate priority clas- sifications was one that generally could not be accom- plished in less than a month to six weeks. After these statements had been received at the WPB, the statistical task involved in arriving at a combined balance sheet for the whole economy was also huge.

During the summer months of 1942 almost the entire staff of the War Production Board struggled heroically to put the Production Requirements Plan into effect. Each industry branch had the task of checking and ap- proving the statements of the various factories under its jurisdiction. The approved statements were then passed on to David Novick, the comptroller of the WPB, who was given the job of compiling the totals.

Novick, a professional statistician of outstanding abil- ity, realized that he could not handle this huge statisti- cal task with the small staff available to him. As a result, he arranged to have the Bureau of the Census take on the job of compilation. The latter organization, of course, had the experience, manpower, and machinery necessary for the assignment.

Finally, around the middle of August, the total re quirements for the large list of materials began to filter through to the Program Adjustment Committee. Almost immediately it was evident that total stated require- ments were far in excess of the anticipated supply of materials available for fourth quarter production. But, where and how to cut back requirements was a puzzle of the first magnitude. If we merely eliminated all re- quests of relatively low priority ratings we had no means of ascertaining what programs, military or civilian, might be affected. There was no possible way of relat- ing a given level of priority rating to any final programs.

During the waning days of August, while we strug- gled with the problem, we became increasingly aware of growing resentment on the part of the military agencies. By now they were convinced that enforcement of the Production Requirements Plan would result in a chaotic situation in the scheduling of their programs, because of the absence of any correlation between priority ratings and military requirements. They were just as much in the dark in this respect as was our group in the WPB.

This resentment reached the boiling point early in September and broke out into an open revolt. At the time Jim Knowlson was off on a two-week fishing trip to Canada in search of a badly needed rest. In his absence I was left as acting chairman of the Requirements Committee and in charge of the whole Program Division. Suddenly I learned that the top military brass had persuaded Don Nelson to abandon the PRP in favor of a vertical plan of allocations which they favored. They also convinced Nelson that, in order to make the new

James S. Knowlson, Program Vice-Chairman
of the War Production Board,
and Vice-Chairman of
the Combined Production and Resources Board,
being awarded the Medal of Merit
by Secretary of War Patterson
in 1946

plan effective, Knowlson should be replaced by Ferdinand Eberstadt as Program Vice-Chairman.

Eberstadt, a prominent investment banker from New York, had been serving up to this time as civilian chairman of the Army-Navy Munitions Board. In this capacity one of his tasks was to coordinate the procurement of munitions for both the Army and the Navy. In addition to being an intimate friend of Jim Forrestal, then serving as Under-Secretary of the Navy, Eberstadt had impressed all of the top military officials with his outstanding abilities.

The news of this shift burst like a bombshell amongst the staff of the Program Division. The whole move took place during Knowlson's absence from Washington, and he only learned of it as a fait accompli on his return to the city late in September. I have always believed that the putsch was deliberately planned to take place while Jim was away. After his removal as Program Vice-Chairman Knowlson devoted his activities entirely to the work of the Combined Production and Resources Board, of which he had been made Vice-Chairman some three months earlier.

The abortive attempt to implement the Production Requirements Plan produced at least one constructive result. The compilation of total demand for materials proved conclusively to everyone that military orders on the books of American plants were in the aggregate far in excess of the industrial capacity of the nation. As a consequence, it was clear that some emergency step would have to be taken in the interim between the abandonment of the PRP and the installation of a new system of allocations.

Under the prodding of his associates, Don Nelson was finally persuaded to issue late in 1942 a special directive to Admiral Leahy, the chairman of the Joint Chiefs of

Staff. This directive ordered a cutback of 20 percent in total orders for military hardware for the calendar year of 1943. The order left to the discretion of the Joint Chiefs the decision as to where such cutbacks should be made as long as the overall reduction added up to the stipulated percentage figure. As anticipated, the Joint Chiefs were unable to agree as to any selective cuts amongst the several agencies. The final result, therefore, was a flat reduction of 20 percent for each agency. This cutback provided an important period of relief from the intolerable pressures of demand during the early months of 1943, and made possible a smoother transition to a permanent system of allocations.

The removal of Jim Knowlson as Program Vice-Chairman of the WPB ended our wartime association. It seems appropriate at this point, therefore, to set forth a brief appraisal of the man and his abilities. First of all, Jim was always a great and good friend to me. He sponsored me in Washington, pushed me ahead, and always supported me loyally in every crisis, large or small.

Jim Knowlson was a graduate of Cornell University and had spent all of his adult life in manufacturing. He was president and chief owner of a little company called the Speedway Manufacturing Company, a maker of tools, until some time in the middle Thirties. At this point he was called in to become president of the ailing Stewart-Warner Corporation. For many years he did a highly successful job of running both companies. The financial health of Stewart-Warner was promptly restored and was set on a path of further growth and expansion. For almost ten years—up to his death in 1959 —I was associated with Knowlson as a director of Stewart-Warner.

Jim was close to sixty years of age in 1942. He had a fine urbane mind and a keen sardonic sense of humor.

Although Knowlson was always a pleasure to work with, it should be added that he lacked some of the dynamic qualities of leadership possessed by his successor, Eberstadt. He did not have the same incisive ability to cut right to the heart of a problem, nor equal administrative talents in knitting together a large organization into a smoothly working team. Nevertheless, I shall always look back with gratitude and affection upon my associations and friendship with James S. Knowlson.

The
evolution
of the
Requirements
Committee

Chapter v I I

I I
The
Controlled Materials
Plan

Ferdinand Eberstadt, without any doubt, was the ablest man with whom I was associated during my years in Washington. This judgment, I may add, was not one that I reached easily. I had known Ferd casually for some years, both in investment banking circles and as a prominent alumnus of Princeton University. I must confess to some prejudice against him when I first learned of his coming to the WPB. I remember remarking to one of my associates: "Eberstadt is certain to dig his own grave here as a result of his driving ambition."

How radically I changed this opinion is disclosed in the following pages. I shall never forget our first interview. As soon as he was installed in the WPB, I went to his office where the following dialogue took place:

Myself:—"Ferd, you have inherited me as your deputy. I am sure you will want someone to whom you are closer and in whom you have greater confidence in this position. I just came here to tell you that I am prepared to step aside whenever you want me to do so. Since a war is going on, however, I shall be glad to stay on here as long as you feel I can be of any service to you."

Eberstadt:—"John, I shall make no promises to you whatsoever. Please just continue what you are now doing. If at any time I want to replace you, I shall be the first to tell you. In the meanwhile don't believe anything you may hear from anyone else."

From this forthright starting point we began to work in harness together. As the weeks passed my admiration for Ferd mounted steadily. The keenness of his mind, his organizational ability, his willingness to make himself available to members of his staff at any time day or night all combined to lift the whole organization to a fine pitch of enthusiasm.

I am equally sure that Eberstadt's confidence in me grew likewise. He gave me more and more authority in handling allocation problems and backed me strongly in my decisions. He arranged to have our division converted into the Program Bureau, of which he made me Director. In the Washington hierarchy, a bureau has a high rank in the Civil Service echelons, and this move not only gave greater prestige to our organization but also made it possible for all of us to receive higher salaries.

The Program Bureau had a small but very able staff of relatively young men. I have already referred to Bill Black, vice-chairman of the Program Adjustment Committee until he left us in the fall of 1942. Mention has also been made of Charlie Kohlhepp, who succeeded Black as vice-chairman of the PAC, and later took on the job as director of the Program Bureau when I resigned in June of 1943. Other key figures included Bertrand Fox and Lincoln Gordon who must be singled out for special praise. Fox was our chief statistician and did a brilliant job of analyzing the requirements of the several claimant agencies. Gordon was particularly effective in special trouble shooting jobs. Much later in the war Linc Gordon became Program Vice-Chairman of the WPB. As previously mentioned, Fred Roe served as secretary of the Requirements Committee, and Charlie Capek as secretary of the PAC.

In addition, I had three special assistants to perform all kinds of miscellaneous tasks that threatened constantly to swamp my office. These were: Arthur (Ted) Wadsworth, a brilliant young investment banker from Dillon, Reed & Co., Bill Day, an equally outstanding young man on leave from the American Telephone & Telegraph Co., and James Ward, a life-long friend of mine from Kansas City. Finally, Blackwell Smith served for a while as another assistant until he left on some special mission to Australia in the fall of 1942.

The plan of allocations which Eberstadt brought with him from the military agencies was known as the Controlled Materials Plan. It had the basically simple theory that the wartime economy could be controlled by making allocations to end-products programs of four essential materials; steel, aluminum, copper and brass. Actually, the plan dealt with five materials because carbon steel and alloy steel were allocated separately. Under the plan, each claimant agency was required to present to the Program Bureau its programmed requirements for a calendar quarter, translated into so many tons of each of the Controlled Materials needed. These stated requirements were submitted first to the several branches of the WPB which had jurisdiction over each of the Controlled Materials. Here they were checked, chiefly for the accuracy of the translation of the end-products program into stated tonnages of the Controlled Materials.

The requirements were than passed on to the statistical section of the Program Bureau. Here the totals were compiled, and each program was analyzed from the standpoint of internal consistency, and in order to bring out any possible discrepancies from the known programs of the several claimant agencies. Thus, when the

Ferdinand Eberstadt, Program Vice-Chairman of the War Production Board, 1942-1943, as he appeared at the time

programmed requirements reached the Program Adjustment Committee, they carried with them the comments and criticisms of the industry branches and of the statistical section. Concurrently, the PAC was furnished with statements of the anticipated supply for the corresponding calendar quarter of each of the Controlled Materials. The estimates of supply were provided by the several WPB branches which were involved.

When the Controlled Materials Plan was introduced, the War Production Board avoided the mistake that was made in connection with PRP of failing to allow sufficient time for advance planning and preparation. First, the plan was scrutinized carefully for several weeks before announcement was made on November 3, 1942 of its official adoption by the WPB. Second, the announcement stated that the plan would not be made fully effective prior to the second quarter of 1943. This schedule allowed ample time for the gathering of bills of materials and the translation of the programs into the tonnages of the Controlled Materials needed to complete them. It also permitted the Program Bureau to gain the invaluable experience of making allocations on a dry-run basis for the first quarter of 1943.

When, as chairman of the Program Adjustment Committee, I was first confronted with the problem of making over-all allocations, I was appalled by the task. To my horror I discovered that total stated requirements for the first quarter of 1943 amounted to almost 200 percent of estimated supplies. Momentarily it seemed an almost impossible job to bring supply and demand into balance. Nevertheless, we settled down to the work of whittling away at the programs of each of the claimant agencies by means of almost daily meetings of the PAC.

I established the procedure of tackling first the allocations of carbon steel, the need for which was common to all of the programs. At the outset we worked on the non-military programs to see how far we could go in cutting them back without endangering the productive capacity of the nation. This was an agonizing process, not because of the fear of imposing hardships on the civilian population, but because of the recognized necessity of maintaining the efficiency of our factories, our railroads and other means of transportation, such as trucks, passenger cars, pipelines, etc. Despite the expressed fears of the claimants involved, we were able to make deep cuts in all of the civilian programs without any serious consequences.

Next we tackled the requirements of what might be called the semi-military programs, such as those of the Lend-Lease Administration, the Board of Economic Warfare, and the Maritime Commission. I was particularly ruthless in cutting back the requests of the Board of Economic Warfare which supervised the requirements of the Latin American nations. Because I had little sympathy for the position of Latin America in the global war I approved only those programs which had a direct relationship to the raw material needs of the United States, such as the iron ore and rubber projects in Brazil. Substantial, though less drastic, cuts were also made in the requests of the Lend-Lease Administration and of the Maritime Commission.

By the time we reached the military agencies we discovered that cutbacks of these latter programs of approximately 30 percent would bring total demand to not more than 110 percent of anticipated supply. We chose this figure as our goal rather than striving for an absolute balance. We did this on the theory, later proved correct, that it was desirable to keep a certain amount of pressure on our productive facilities. In addition, we recognized that an unknown amount of stated requirements were likely to become lost in the shuffle as a result of delays in scheduling and for other reasons.

As far as carbon steel was concerned, we had no particular problem in connection with the requirements of the Air Force. Its needs for this material were relatively small. The primary requirements of the Air Force were for aluminum sheets and alloy steel, the former for air frames, and the latter for aircraft engines and airborne equipment. Under the Presidential Aircraft Program, the Air Force had first call on aluminum and alloy steel, and no one dared interfere with this program. The special problems that arose in connection with the aircraft program are discussed in some detail in a later chapter.

Thus, we were finally faced with the necessity of making cuts of about 30 percent in the combined programs of the Army and the Navy. We, in the Program Bureau, did not have the temerity to suggest selective cuts as between the two agencies, particularly since we knew that the Joint Chiefs of Staff had never been able to cope successfully with this problem. As a result, we finally decided to make equal and arbitrary cuts in both programs.

I was never greatly concerned that such cutbacks would result in the emasculation of any essential military programs. In the first place, I was confident that the military requirements were deliberately padded in anticipation of cutbacks. In the second place, we knew that both programs contained marginal requests which could be dropped without any serious effect on the over-all war effort. Thus, the Navy was forced to abandon its demands for a huge floating dry dock, which it proposed to tow out to the South Pacific, and for two heavily armored target ships. In place of the target ships, we suggested to the Navy that it do its target practice on the Japanese. Similarly, the Army was forced to reduce its program for what we called the Army's navy, a group of special ships for which no urgent need was seen.

When a balance had been achieved between the demand and the supply of carbon steel, allocations of the other Controlled Materials became much easier to handle. I have already mentioned the special position of the Air Force in relation to aluminum and alloy steel. In the case of copper and brass, there were certain urgent civilian demands. Copper was badly needed for electrical wiring throughout the economy, and the railroads had to have large amounts of brass to maintain the bearing journals of freight car axles. Nevertheless, we were able to allocate to the Armed Services sufficient amounts of these two materials to carry out all of their essential programs.

I made it my job to keep Eberstadt fully informed of the daily progress made by the Program Adjustment Committee. We both regarded this as essential so that he, as the final arbiter of allocations, would be in accord with the decisions being made at the level of the PAC. The result of this close liaison was that final approval of the allocations by the Requirements Committee became little more than a formality.

The task of making allocations under the Controlled Materials Plan became progressively easier with the passage of each succeeding quarter. Stated requirements were more and more in line with the realities of available supply. Thus, total demands for the second quarter of 1943 were 175 percent of supply as compared with almost 200 percent in the first quarter. When we were ready to make allocations for the third quarter we found that total requirements were not more than 150 percent of supply. By this time it was clear that non-military requirements had been pared down to minimum levels essential for the maintenance of an efficient operating economy. As a result, the allocation problem became largely one of making arbitrary, across-the-board cuts in the military demands.

The Controlled Materials Plan represented a tremendous step forward from the abortive attempt to put the Production Requirements Plan into operation. The plan was easy to understand; it did not overwhelm everyone with an impossible mass of paperwork; and it was relatively simple to operate. Each claimant agency had control of its own programs within the limits of the materials allocated to it. It could schedule these programs with full knowledge of what it was doing, and with confidence that production would be accomplished in accordance with plans.

Nevertheless, the CMP had certain weaknesses that were almost inevitable in any simple scheme designed to control a vast and complex economy such as that of the United States. The chief weakness resulted from the basic assumption of the plan that there would be a one-for-one correlation between the supply of raw materials and the fabricating capacity necessary to convert these materials into finished products. This, as we soon discovered, was not the case. Bottlenecks began to appear in what were known as common components—heat exchangers, electric motors, valves, etc., which were badly needed in many different programs.

The most interesting lesson that I learned of the lack of a perfect correlation between the supply of a raw material and finishing capacity came not in the field of common components but in the case of steel bars for reinforcing cement. The production of such bars had been prohibited at an earlier date by the War Production Board. In the second quarter of 1943, Joe Block, head of the Iron and Steel Branch, came to me to request my approval for the production of a moderate amount of such reinforcing bars. At first I had almost a closed mind against such a request. Finally, after a long discussion, Joe convinced me that the relationship between raw steel ingot production and finishing capacity was so geared together that ingot production would exceed total finishing capacity unless a moderate tonnage of ingots were converted into reinforcing bars. Once I had this truth firmly fixed in my mind, I approved his request. What this meant, of course, was that the amount of steel available for end-products programs was determined by the steel finishing capacity of the nation rather than by the supply of raw ingots. As one moved up the ladder of fabrication and subassemblies similar bottlenecks were uncovered.

After hours and weeks of discussion and arguments a compromise solution was introduced to break the bottleneck in the production of common components. All products which came under the Controlled Materials Plan were divided into two classifications. The primary group was called "A" products, such as tanks, guns, ships, bombs, trucks, etc., against which allocations could be made directly by the Requirements Committee. A second group called "B" products was made up of specially designated common components which were known to be in short supply. Materials for the manufacture of these "off-the-shelf" items were allocated directly to the factories producing them in the horizontal manner of the Production Requirements Plan. Under this system, component manufacturers were able to go all out in their production with full confidence that the necessary materials would be available. As these components were in turn incorporated into the end-products programs, the controlled materials consumed by the component manufacturers were charged against the allocated quotas of the several claimant agencies.

With this one important modification the Controlled Materials Plan continued in operation throughout the emergency. In my opinion, it was as efficient a method of making allocations and of controlling our complex economy as could be devised. It had the virtues of being simple to understand, and relatively easy to operate. I only hope that if, and when, our country should be faced with a similar emergency the lessons learned in World War II will not be forgotten. It certainly should be unnecessary again to spend months of fumbling and agonizing in order to establish an adequate system of controls for another wartime economy.

During the Eberstadt regime, the Requirements Committee and the Program Bureau became the hub of the whole War Production Board, around which everything else tended to revolve. As time passed, we were called upon to review a wide variety of allocation problems. Many of these problems related to the Controlled Materials Plan, but some had no connection whatsoever.

In the former category I remember sitting one whole day listening to a presentation by the staff of the Petroleum Administrator for War. This agency made a fervent plea for a much larger allocation of steel for drill pipe because of an alleged danger of exhausting our domestic oil reserves. If my memory serves me correctly, our proven reserves at that time were given at 12 billion barrels, equivalent at the then prevailing rate of consumption to about eight years' supply.

I was not greatly impressed by the arguments of the Petroleum Administration because I had heard similar scare stories in the past regarding the danger of exhausting our oil reserves. Also, I felt that, if there ever was a time when we would be justified in pulling down our oil reserves, it would be in the middle of an all-out war. As a result, the Office of the Petroleum Administrator obtained very little satisfaction from the Program Bureau. In this connection it is interesting to observe that, while consumption of crude oil in the United States has increased by only 50 percent since World War II, proven oil reserves have almost quadrupled.

In the category of problems far removed from the Controlled Materials Plan, I remember particularly those relating to lumber and fish. The problem of allocating the supply of lumber from Canada as well as from the United States had become very involved, and the Lumber Branch of the WPB came to the Program Bureau for advice and help. I cannot recall that we were able to render any very constructive assistance but I know that we spent a good deal of time struggling with the problem.

Similarly, the Food Administration came to us for advice in allocating the supply of fish between the United States and Great Britain. An amusing aspect of this problem arose in connection with menhaden, a fish of the herring family which was in abundant supply along our Atlantic Coast. Ordinarily this fish is used for bait, oil and fertilizer, but not for human consumption. The British were badly in need of high protein supplements to their diet but refused our offer to let them have a large supply of menhaden. Subsequently, some bright young man in the Food Administration had the brilliant idea of rechristening these fish with the name "Silver Herring". Under this disguise, the British gladly accepted the whole supply.

I shall close this chapter with a brief anecdote regarding the labor unions and the Requirements Committee. One day in January 1943, a group of about 50 labor union officials descended on Washington with the idea of learning something of the work of the War Production Board. The group met in the large auditorium of the Social Security Building and were addressed by a series of officials on different aspects of the WPB.

At Eberstadt's request, I appeared before these labor leaders to describe the functioning of the Requirements Committee. Just as I was well launched in my talk, I was interrupted by Walter Reuther who occupied a seat in the first row. He sprang to his feet, turned his back on me and made an impassioned address to his colleagues as to the necessity of having labor represented on the Requirements Committee. I continued talking to the back of his neck, but his voice was louder than my own. I am afraid I never succeeded in getting across my simple message that membership on the Requirements Committee was restricted to the agencies which were the chief consumers of essential materials and that in no way could organized labor be classified as a claimant agency. I finally gave up in disgust and left the group still discussing amongst themselves the merits of Reuther's plea.

The eviction of Eberstadt

When Ferd Eberstadt came to the War Production Board he took what he felt were essential precautions to make certain that his position as Program Vice Chair man could not be undermined by the New Dealers. Thus, he insisted upon, and was granted, complete control over all the industry branches of the WPB. With such control he was confident that no one could run around his end and nullify the effectiveness of the Controlled Materials Plan.

Unfortunately, he failed to reckon with the ingenuity of his enemies. Almost immediately Don Nelson and his New Deal cronies began to make plans designed to undermine the influence of Eberstadt. The rationale of this group was that the WPB, and indeed the national economy, was now in serious danger of being dominated by

65

the military agencies. As a first step in this campaign, Nelson decided to create a new office in the War Production Board which would serve as a counterweight to the position of Eberstadt.

Thus, the office of Production Vice-Chairman was established in the fall of 1942, and Charles Wilson, President of General Electric, was called to Washington by President Roosevelt to occupy this post. I am sure that Charlie Wilson entered the job in all innocence as to what his real role in the New Deal scheme of things was intended to be. He was told that his function was to be the supervision and control of production scheduling by the military agencies. Soon after his arrival he discovered that he had a high-sounding title but no actual authority because all of the industry branches of the WPB were under the direct control of Eberstadt, and because the military authorities were wholly unwilling to turn over to any outsider the control of their production schedules.

During the next couple of months Wilson searched for ways to make himself useful, but became increasingly restive in a position that gave him no direct authority or responsibility. Finally, around the end of December, 1942, Charlie advised Roosevelt that, unless he could be given some real responsibility, he would have no alternative but to return to his position at General Electric. The result was that the President ordered Don Nelson to turn over to Wilson control over the aircraft and aluminum branches of the WPB.

The announcement of this shift was shattering to Eberstadt and the rest of us in the Program Bureau. We all realized that such a division of authority, particularly in the critical areas of aircraft and aluminum, could nullify the effectiveness of the whole system of allocations. Ferd asked me to accompany him to Nelson's office in order to lodge a strong protest against the proposed action. It was a brief but illuminating interview. After listening to our arguments for a few minutes, Nelson, looking like a whipped dog, said plaintively: "Eber, I know it is just as wrong as you say it is. I can only ask you to believe me that I had no choice in the matter."

From this point on the fat was in the fire. A cleavage had been created in the WPB which could only widen and deepen with the passage of time. Whether they liked it or not, Eberstadt and Wilson were placed in positions of mutual antagonism which became progressively more bitter. During January and early February of 1943 rumors grew steadily as to an impending shake-up in the leadership of the War Production Board.

About the middle of February it became apparent that something would have to give. Newspaper columnists were aware of the rift and were giving the matter increasing publicity. Finally, on Friday morning, February 13, an inspired article in the New York Times reported that Eberstadt was scheduled to be ousted from the WPB. The following morning a second inspired article appeared in the Washington Post which stated dogmatically that Donald Nelson was scheduled for removal.

During these days I had no part in the hectic discussions and negotiations that were taking place, and knew nothing of actual developments in the battle. At the time I was deeply involved in working out the basic allocations for the second quarter of the year. I thought it the part of wisdom to keep my mouth shut and ask no questions.

The first intimation I received of a break in the fierce struggle came early on Monday morning, February 16, following the appearance of the inspired newspaper articles referred to above. Eberstadt called me to his office and said: "I just wanted to tell you to keep your shirt on. Everything is going to work out fine." My only reply was: "Okay, boss, that's wonderful," and promptly returned to my office.

Ferd had called a meeting of the top military brass at ten that morning to discuss the knotty problem of allocating common components, already discussed in some detail in the preceding chapter. In attendance, in addition to Eberstadt and myself, were General Clay for the Army, General Hopkins for the Air Force, Admiral Robinson for the Navy, and Admiral Land for the Maritime Commission.

About ten-thirty, Eberstadt's secretary entered the meeting room and handed him a note on a slip of paper. After reading the message, Ferd whispered to me: "I have just received an urgent call to go to Nelson's office. Please carry on and run the meeting until I get back."

The discussion dragged on for two and a half hours with no sign of Eberstadt. Finally at one P.M., I said: "Well, gentlemen, I am afraid there's no use in waiting any longer for Ferd. I suggest we break up and have lunch."

When we emerged into the large outside corridor we found it filled with people, shouting and gesticulating in their anxiety to tell us the news. We learned (1) that Eberstadt had been summarily fired by Nelson on the grounds of disloyalty to his chief; (2) that Nelson had delegated all his powers to Charlie Wilson and given the latter the title of Executive Vice-Chairman of the WPB; and (3) that Nelson had immediately given the story to reporters and the news was already in the papers. We also learned that Eberstadt had been so angry and disgusted that he had walked straight out of the building without even bothering to return to his office for his hat and overcoat.

It was not until two days later that I learned from Lucius Clay the actual sequence of events that had transpired over this momentous weekend. First, I was advised that President Roosevelt a few days earlier had written a letter to Bernard Baruch, the well-known elder statesman of the Democratic Party, and offered him the position as Chairman of the War Production Board in place of Nelson. The understanding was that Ferdinand Eberstadt would be named as Baruch's deputy and would be given all the authority to administer the entire organization. Second, the President had planned to announce this change on Monday afternoon, February 16.

Sometime during the preceding evening, the news of the impending development was leaked by a member of the White House staff to Robert Nathan, one of Nelson's closest New Deal advisors. Nathan promptly called Nelson and arranged to join him for breakfast the following morning, along with several of his other close advisors. At this early morning meeting Nelson was advised substantially as follows:

"Boss, your goose is cooked unless you take immediate and drastic action. It is possible that you may save yourself if you take certain steps before you have been advised officially of the Presidential decision. Call in Eberstadt at once and fire him as a traitor to you; then delegate all of your authority to Charlie Wilson, and release the news immediately to the press. Under such circumstances, you will have created a situation that not even the President of the United States will dare to upset."

Nelson did as advised and the result was exactly as predicted. Not only did Roosevelt fail to upset the coup d'état, but actually he wrote by hand that afternoon a letter to Donald Nelson congratulating him on his courage in firing Eberstadt—this to a man whom he had agreed to remove on that same day. It is a story of palace intrigue that I still find difficult to accept after the passage of twenty years. If it had appeared in the pages of E. Phillips Oppenheim, I am sure almost everyone would agree that such a series of events simply could not happen in the Twentieth Century United States of America.

Thus ended my wartime association with Ferdinand Eberstadt. I have already expressed my admiration for his great abilities and do not need to repeat them here. I have always felt that no one in his right mind could be critical of the masterful way in which Eberstadt administered allocations and brought the national economy into balance for an all-out war effort. Consequently, I am confident that the New Deal attack against him was motivated by the belief that he was the tool of the military, and that through him the Armed Services would control the nation.

Moreover, I am certain there was no real justification for this fear. Ferd was at all times his own master and was not the tool of anyone. He was just as ready to crack down on the Armed Services if they stepped out of bounds as he was in the case of any other agency. It was merely his misfortune that his position in the War Production Board had been sponsored primarily by military chieftains.

That his real abilities were recognized by Democratic leaders was demonstrated by the fact that he was called back to Washington by President Truman in 1947. When the outlines of the Cold War with Russia began to emerge, Eberstadt was asked to prepare plans for a mobilization of the national economy in the event the Cold War should become hot. He spent several months at this task and, at Ferd's request, I also went to Washington for a brief period to assist him in making these plans. In addition, Eberstadt played an important role as a member of the Hoover Commission in its study and report on the Defense Department.

A final, though unacknowledged, tribute to Eberstadt was the fact that the machinery he had established for the making of allocations was left practically unchanged by his successors. The Controlled Materials Plan remained in force as long as there was need for a tight control over the national economy.

The eviction of Eberstadt

The
aftermath

My immediate inclination, after learning the full circumstances surrounding Eberstadt's dismissal, was to resign from the War Production Board, and to remove myself as far as possible from this hotbed of intrigue. I quickly realized, however, that this might not be an easy step to take. We were still in the middle of a global war, and I did not feel I could justify at this time a return to the investment banking business. My conscience informed me that I would have to find some other form of activity that was related to the national war effort.

Two days after the removal of Eberstadt I was invited by Lucius Clay to have lunch with him in the Pentagon. It was here that I learned the details of the dramatic events of the preceding weekend. When I told him of my desire to resign from the WPB, Clay urged me as a favor to the Armed Services to stay on at least until the third quarter allocations had been completed, and thus provide a continuity of administration for the Controlled Materials Plan. Coming from a man whom I admired as much as General Clay, it was a request I could not refuse.

Meanwhile Julius A. Krug had been appointed to succeed Eberstadt as Program Vice-Chairman. "Cap" Krug was a large stout man, a few years younger than I. Prior to the war he had served as chief engineer of the Tennessee Valley Authority. During the first fifteen months of the war he was head of the Office of War Utilities, the branch of the WPB that handled the requirements of the public utilities of the country. It is my understanding that he performed this task with distinction.

I had no difficulty in working with Krug. He was a man of quiet strength and dignity. My only complaint was that he did not make himself readily available to the staff of the Program Bureau. In a way, however, this proved to be something of a blessing because he gave me an almost completely free hand in working out the allocation problems. Krug and I had no arguments whatsoever, and the allocations for the third quarter were put into effect with a minimum of difficulties.

As we moved into the months of April and May it became increasingly clear to me that the major task of the Requirements Committee had been accomplished. Except for the continuing problem of common components the Controlled Materials Plan was working smoothly, and the economy was in balance. Already a number of small surpluses had begun to appear in some surprising places. The first of these was in the supply of magnesium, that strange white metal that produced the fire bombs that devastated Tokyo. Next, as soon as aircraft engine production was brought into line with air-frame output, we discovered that we had a surplus of alloy steel. All of these factors helped to convince me that the time was approaching when I could move on to some other activity with a clear conscience.

A way out was provided for me in May by Paul Hoffman, then president of the Studebaker Corporation. I had been closely associated with Paul in the financing of Studebaker prior to the war, and he had become the godfather of my son. Early in 1943 he had organized a nationwide group of businessmen to make plans for a smooth reconversion of the economy to a peacetime basis when the war had ended. This organization was called the Committee for Economic Development and Hoffman was its first chairman.

Paul called on me early in May at the War Production Board and urged me to become the Executive Director of the newly formed CED. Because this job seemed a satisfactory alternative to my work at the WPB, I accepted with the proviso that I would first have to complete the task of making the allocations for the third quarter. This chore was finished by the end of May, and I entered my new position early in June with an office in the Department of Commerce building in Washington.

Before I left the WPB, however, I received an unusual proposal from the Under Secretary of State, Sumner Welles. A letter reached me about the middle of May signed "Welles", scrawled across the bottom of the page in letters at least two inches high. It had all the appearance and manner of an imperial command. The letter requested me to undertake a special mission for the State Department. The proposal was that I make an escorted tour to all the principal Latin American countries. The objective was to have me prepare a study of the wartime requirements of Latin America, and, on my

return, present my conclusions to the War Production
Board.

The offer was a very tempting one. I realized the proposed junket would be an exceedingly interesting experience, and probably never again would I have an opportunity to see these countries under such favorable
auspices. Nevertheless, I realized almost immediately
that I could not accept the proposal. The day following
my receipt of the letter I was called on by an emissary
of the Under Secretary who urged me to undertake the
mission. I gave him my answer in the following words:

"You know I take a very dim view of the position of
Latin America in this war. As I see it, they are sitting on
the sidelines and growing rich while we and the British
are doing their fighting for them. If I should take this
trip I should do so with a fairly closed mind. I would be
wined and dined lavishly in all the capitals. Then, when
I returned and refused to recommend that a single
pound more of strategic materials be allocated to Latin
America, our friends south of the border would have
every right to regard me as the kind of stinker that I
may be anyway."

After my departure from the WPB I was able to keep
in close touch with developments during the succeeding
months through my many good friends who were still
with that organization. Thus, I learned during the summer of 1943 that relations between Donald Nelson and
Charlie Wilson, the new executive vice-chairman, were
deteriorating rapidly. Apparently Nelson, having delegated all his powers to Wilson, became restive from the
lack of much to do, and attempted to reassert some of
his former authority. This naturally was resented by
Wilson. Next, Don became interested in the problems of
reconversion of the economy after the war's end, and
attempted to make some moves in this direction.

This effort by Nelson was resisted violently both by Wilson and by the armed services. The latter were unanimous in their conviction that any announcement of reconversion plans by the WPB, while the war was raging all over the world, would have a seriously adverse effect on the morale of the workers in the war plants. They had no quarrel with the work of independent businessmen, such as the CED, making plans for reconversion. They felt, however, that any indication of a relaxation of controls by the War Production Board might have a disastrous effect on our war effort.

The battle between Nelson and Wilson became so embittered by the fall of 1943 that Sidney Weinberg was called back to Washington to act as an intermediary between the two men. Weinberg, the senior partner of Goldman, Sachs & Co. in New York, was a good friend of both Nelson and Wilson, having served for years on the boards of Sears, Roebuck and General Electric. During the first year of the war Weinberg had performed an outstanding job for the WPB in recruiting top business personnel for the organization.

The next development of importance was the resignation of Cap Krug as Program Vice-Chairman some time around the end of the year. Krug resigned from the WPB in order to take a commission in the Navy.

Shortly after the announcement of Krug's withdrawal, I received a call from Charlie Wilson asking me to visit him at his office. When I did so I found Charlie occupying an office at one end of a vast reception room. Nelson's office was at the other end, and I gathered that the two men were communicating with each other only through Sidney Weinberg.

Wilson urged me to return to the WPB and take the position vacated by Krug as Program Vice-Chairman. Knowing the situation that existed between the two top men of the WPB, I had no stomach for the idea. The final clincher that made me turn down the proposal was a statement made by Wilson. He admitted in our conversation that the allocations problem had become so routinized that he could not attach much significance to the future role of the Program Vice-Chairman. This meeting marked my last official contact with the War Production Board.

During the succeeding months the row between Nelson and Wilson became so serious that it broke out into the press. Finally, in the summer of 1944, President Roosevelt felt compelled to take action. Nelson was sent off to China on a special mission; Wilson returned to his position as president of General Electric; and Krug was recalled from the Navy to become Chairman of the War Production Board.

Meanwhile, in the usual pattern of the New Deal bureaucracy, a new super-agency was created and imposed on top of the WPB. This was called the Office of War Mobilization and Reconversion, and was placed under the direction of former Supreme Court Justice James Byrnes. Sometime in the late fall of 1944, the President decided to activate this new agency. General Lucius Clay was recalled from France to become the deputy to Jimmy Byrnes and the active operating head of the agency. Clay had been sent abroad shortly after the Normandy invasion to take charge of the vast logistical problem of getting supplies to the invading armies.

Clay's appointment to the OWM brought an unwelcome bit of publicity for me. Shortly after this announcement, one of the well-known New Deal Washington correspondents wrote a piece in his nationally syndicated column about Clay. In speculating as to the appointment of a deputy to General Clay in the OWM,

77

he wrote the following sentence: "Prominently mentioned for this post is the name of John F. Fennelly, a strong anti-labor man from Chicago."

It happened that I had just brought my family back to Chicago preparatory to re-entering my investment banking firm at the year's end. The day following the publication of the column I was besieged by reporters. All I could tell them was that I knew nothing whatsoever about the matter, and that I was in no position to accept such an appointment even if it should be offered to me. Two days later the press carried the news of the appointment of Robert Nathan as deputy to Clay. Nathan, a New Deal economist, had served earlier as head of the planning committee of the War Production Board.

When I read this item a great light burst upon me. Immediately it became clear that the story about me had been deliberately planted by friends of Nathan in an effort to kill off in advance any possibility of my appointment. It was a popular maneuver of the New Deal bureaucracy. It was well known that I was a friend of Clay and perhaps my name had even been mentioned in this connection. In any event, someone felt the need to publicize the idea that I would be an undesirable candidate for the job.

At first I was startled and somewhat shocked to realize that I could be regarded as an "anti-labor man": On reflection, however, I began to understand how I might have acquired such a reputation. First, in my capacity as executive director of the Committee for Economic Development, I had testified before a Senate Committee on the problem of removing wartime controls. Union officials had recommended the immediate removal of wage controls and the maintenance of price controls. Some of them had even urged me to take the same position. This I had refused to do. Instead I recommended the maintenance of full controls until the actual ending of hostilities and then the concurrent removal of both price and wage controls.

Second, in a number of speeches for the CED, I had discussed the proposed Full Employment Act which even in 1944 was under consideration by the Congress. In these talks I had pointed out the serious inflationary dangers of any such legislation. Of course, both of the above positions taken by me were certain to be unpopular with the leaders of organized labor.

Just a few words now about my work with the Committee for Economic Development between June 1943 and November 1944. This organization was an offshoot of the Business Advisory Council of the Secretary of Commerce. The Secretary, Jesse Jones, became concerned early in 1943 about the immense problems of reconversion after the war's end. The immediate demobilization of the millions of men and women of the armed forces and the transfer of other millions from war plants to peacetime pursuits threatened to create a highly dangerous situation. There were vivid memories of the apple-selling ex-servicemen of the postwar depression years of 1920 and 1921, and every thoughtful citizen was anxious to avoid a repetition of this tragedy.

Mr. Jones and the Business Advisory Council felt that the primary attack on the problem should be through a voluntary group of businessmen with a nationwide organization of local community units. It was to be the task of each local group to develop plans to absorb into industry as many as possible of the vast numbers of individuals suddenly released from the military services and the war plants. All the funds necessary for this effort were to be provided by industry itself. The result was the creation of the Committee for Economic Development with Paul Hoffman as Chairman, William Benton as Vice-Chairman, and myself as Executive Director.

The CED was set up to perform two separate but related tasks. The first was to stimulate community planning for the development of a maximum number of postwar job opportunities. The second was a research activity on the part of the central business group, aided by a number of professional economists, in the field of postwar economic problems. Professor Theodore Yntema, of the University of Chicago, and later of the Ford Motor Company, was the first Director of Research.

The CED was originally designed as a temporary effort which would terminate automatically after the war. Time and again Paul Hoffman in his early speeches described the organization as the only body he had ever known that signed its own death warrant at the time of its birth.

I took this program seriously because to me the work was a patriotic, wartime service and this was the entire extent of my interest.

The idea of developing reconversion plans at the local level caught on like wildfire. Before long every important city in the country had its local CED group working feverishly on postwar plans. These schemes varied widely and many were extremely ingenious. This planning served not only to create many additional job opportunities but also to give to the businessmen of the country a constructive and optimistic approach to the postwar world. In retrospect I am convinced that the work of the CED in this area was an essential factor in making the transition from war to peace a smooth and relatively painless operation.

The work of the national research committee, of

80

which I was a member, was pursued with energy and enthusiasm. I am afraid, however, that the impact of its published studies on the national mind was of minor significance. We worked on postwar problems of taxation, the federal budget, agriculture, small business, etc., and took ourselves very seriously. We looked forward hopefully to postwar federal budgets of not more than 12 to 15 billion dollars and to major reductions in the burden of income taxes. In retrospect this optimism now seems startlingly naive, but, of course, we were unaware at that time that we would move swiftly from a hot war into a cold war with Russia. Perhaps the most important result of the research committee's work was that it provided a postgraduate course in economics for the businessmen involved.

For me the work with the CED was a stimulating and broadening experience. I spent a great deal of time with the research committee, but unfortunately found myself involved almost continuously in ideological arguments with a number of the associated professional economists who were proponents of the Keynesian approach to economics. Also, I travelled extensively throughout the United States and Canada, meeting with local business groups and making speeches on the reconversion philosophy of the CED.

In the fall of 1944 everyone realized that the war was approaching a successful conclusion. Late in September we held an annual meeting of the trustees of the CED at Hot Springs, Virginia. In accordance with the original plan of the organization to fade out of existence with the war's end, I presented a sharply reduced budget of expenditures for the calendar year of 1945. Immediately an outcry arose from all sides protesting against the idea of terminating the life of this wonderful group. I listened incredulously while the enthusiasm for continuing indefinitely the life of the CED rose to a fever pitch. My reduced budget for 1945 was voted down almost unanimously, and a new expanded budget was approved in its stead. Immediately after the meeting I submitted my resignation as Executive Director and returned to Chicago to rejoin Glore, Forgan & Co. at the year's end.

Nevertheless, I continued for several months thereafter as a member of the research committee. I became more and more fed up, however, with the intellectual domination of the business group by the Keynesian economists of the CED staff. This influence was so strong that I felt it was impossible for a traditional economist like myself to play an effective part in the deliberations of the committee. As a result, I resigned from the group early in 1945.

The CED has continued in operation ever since as a research group of distinguished business leaders which periodically publishes reports on current economic problems. It has freed itself from the early left wing influence of certain of the professionals and is today a highly respected organization.

This ends the chronological report of my wartime experiences in Washington. The remaining chapters of the book consist of cross section views of certain aspects of my work and relationships in the War Production Board. My chief regret in connection with this period in my life is that I was unable to accompany General Clay to Germany after the war's end. When General Eisenhower returned from Europe to become Chief of Staff of our Army, Clay succeeded him as Commander of the American Army of Occupation in Germany. Just before he left for Europe, Lucius called me on the phone and urged me to come with him as a member of his staff. I shall always regret that I felt compelled to decline because I am sure it would have been a fascinating experience. I had, however, been absent from my business for almost three full years, and I realized it was high time that I stuck to my job and supported my family. The only alternative would have been to make a permanent career of public service, a life for which I lacked the necessary financial independence.

New Dealers
and
businessmen

One of the most pervasive facts of life in the War Production Board was the never-ending harassment of the business executives in this organization by members of the permanent bureaucracy. The more radical elements of the New Deal office holders resented intensely the intrusion of business leaders into important government posts and were determined to make life miserable for them. This somewhat shadowy and shifting group became known to the WPB staff as "the palace guard of the White House".

It is not possible for me to state how active a part Vice-President Wallace played in this vendetta but it is certain that the other members of the group looked upon him as their spiritual guide and leader. His position in this regard was made clear when the Board of Economic Warfare was created in the fall of 1941 under his titular leadership.

That this new organization was dominated by left wing elements became obvious at an early date. I was called to Washington about two months before Pearl Harbor by Milo Perkins who had just been appointed director of the Board of Economic Warfare under Wallace. Perkins invited me to join his show. He then proceeded to outline the anticipated scope of activity of the Board of Economic Warfare. He stated flatly that it expected gradually to take over most of the foreign policy functions of the State Department.

This fantastic dream died aborning. That old feuding mountaineer from Tennessee, Cordell Hull, was too experienced a hand at warding off left wing attacks on the prerogatives of his State Department. Very promptly Hull saw to it that the activities of the Board were restricted solely to the screening of wartime requirements of the Latin American nations, and this was all done under the supervision of the Department of State. As a result, the Board of Economic Warfare remained throughout the war an enclave of frustrated New Dealers who were limited to a relatively minor part in the overall war effort. Naturally, I refused the invitation to join this group.

It is also difficult to pinpoint with certainty all of the other leading members of the Palace Guard. Four names, however, stand out in my memory. These were: Robert Nathan, New Deal economist who functioned as chairman of the WPB Planning Board; Mordecai Ezekial, of the Department of Agriculture; Edward F. Pritchard, a member of Justice Frankfurter's staff; and Leon Henderson, head of the office of Price Administration. I am confident that these four men were actively involved in the major attacks on the business leadership of the WPB, such as those described in earlier chapters. There were several other individuals in the WPB who were in close contact with this group but whose active participation in the running battle was too doubtful to justify their identification in this story.

Although he undoubtedly aided the Palace Guard at times, I am reasonably sure that Harry Hopkins was not continuously concerned with their intrigues. It is true that Hopkins was primarily responsible for the appointment of Donald Nelson as chairman of the War Production Board in January, 1942. On the other hand, I am sure he was far too busy with his own wartime activities to become involved in the later activities of this group. The same, I am sure, was true of Benjamin Cohen of the White House staff. Cohen, along with Tommy Corcoran, attained nationwide prominence during the early years of the Roosevelt regime as an intimate adviser to the President. During the war years, however, he became relatively aloof from the new crowd of Young Turks.

I remember attending a dinner of New Deal planners in the spring of 1943 to discuss the problems of postwar reconversion of the economy. During the discussions Cohen became involved in an argument with Mordecai Ezekial. The argument ended when Cohen referred contemptuously to what he called "the Ezekial brand of economic fascism".

Although I came to know fairly well most of the left wing group of New Deal bureaucrats, it has always seemed strange to me that I never met, or even heard of, Alger Hiss, during the war years.

What were the basic motives behind the activities of the Palace Guard? In essence I am sure it was part of the unceasing struggle for political power between radicals and conservatives that continued throughout all the years of the Roosevelt Administration. I doubt that the left-wing elements disliked the businessmen much more than they did conservative Democrats like Cordell Hull. They were also constantly fearful that the military would take over control of the economy. Thus, I am confident that the attack that finally overthrew Ferdinand Eberstadt was motivated more by the belief that Eberstadt was a tool of the Armed Services than it was by dislike of him as a businessman.

Of course, the radical group had special reasons for attacking businessmen. In their book of political philosophy every representative of Big Business was automatically classified as a robber baron, who, unless closely watched, would probably try to run off with the United States Treasury. Particular resentment was also felt against the "dollar-a-year" plan, under which business executives were allowed to retain their full business salaries while working for the government.

I have already referred to the fact that Donald Nelson was a darling of the New Dealers. They regarded him with affection because they were confident they could control his policies. This mutual admiration society continued for at least the first eighteen months of the war. It was still in full effect in the spring of 1943 when the Palace Guard prodded Nelson into the expulsion of Ferdinand Eberstadt. Thereafter, however, Nelson's popularity with the New Dealers began to decline. I am sure they had a great deal to do with his eventual replacement as Chairman of the War Production Board by J. A. Krug.

My own relationships with the Palace Guard were somewhat unusual and, from my standpoint, quite fortunate. In the first place, I never occupied a position of sufficient importance to mark me as a prime target for attack. Beyond this, however, my academic background provided me with a unique protective coloration. Because of my Ph.D. and my associations with Columbia University most of the New Dealers regarded me as one of their own kind rather than as a business executive. Finally, the fact that I was living solely on a small government salary marked me in their minds as something different from the usual run of businessmen.

Moreover, I had in the ranks of the New Dealers an intimate friend and adviser. Tom Blaisdell, who had occupied several different governmental posts since the early days of Roosevelt, had formerly shared an office with me when we were both instructors at Columbia University. As a member of the WPB Planning Board during the war, Blaisdell was closely identified with the Palace Guard. He was, however, too much of a gentleman to become actively involved in the internecine warfare.

I always went to Tom for guidance in my dealings with the New Deal bureaucracy. He gave me unfailingly honest advice as to those individuals I could trust and those of whom I should be wary. I am sure he was always a staunch friend at court for me in New Deal circles.

Shortly after the war I was able to repay in some small measure my debt of gratitude to Tom Blaisdell. At that time he was serving as Assistant Secretary of Commerce under Harry Truman. Tom had the misfortune to employ a communist follower by the name of Elizabeth Bentley. Because of this he was brought before a Loyalty Investigating Board. At Tom's request I wrote a strong letter to the Board testifying to his patriotism and integrity. Blaisdell was completely exonerated by the Board. Shortly thereafter, however, he resigned from government service and since then he has served as a professor at the University of California.

The net result of all the above was that I was almost completely immune from attack by the Palace Guard during my stay in the War Production Board. I did learn later that I was under suspicion by this group during the months when I served as deputy to Ferdinand Eberstadt. Thus, I was advised that the telephone wires to my office had been tapped for several weeks prior to the eviction of Eberstadt. Apparently nothing damaging to me was learned from the monitoring of the innumerable telephone conversations I must have had, because I never heard anything more about the matter.

Professors and businessmen

Probably because I had spent parts of my life in both fields I was intensely interested in observing the relative abilities of business executives on the one hand and of the academicians on the other in wartime Washington. The War Production Board had a large quota of college professors in its ranks, as did most of the other wartime agencies. These individuals were automatically classified as New Dealers by the business groups, but in a great many instances such was not the case. For the most part the academicians were simply men of good will who had come to Washington to render service to their country in a global war.

With a few notable exceptions, such as Ferdinand Eberstadt, I finally had to conclude that the professors as a group showed the greater understanding of governmental machinery and greater flexibility in adapting themselves to the peculiar intricacies of bureaucratic red tape. I suspect also that their training had prepared them better for the broad scope of the problems involved in controlling a wartime economy.

In making this somewhat invidious comparison, I am considering only those men who were working at the levels of planning and policy making. Excluded are the large group of devoted businessmen who ran the many industry branches of the WPB. I am fully aware that many of the latter group performed outstanding jobs for their respective industries. As a shining example of such performance I think of Joe Block, (Joseph L. Block, chairman of Inland Steel), who managed the affairs of the Iron and Steel Branch with great efficiency.

The typical business executive, however, (if, indeed, there is any such animal) found himself in a world that was very alien to his previous business experiences. He was confused by the winds of political controversy, by the struggles of power amongst the different agencies of the government, and by the many executive orders, each of which tended to conflict with the directives set forth in the others. The business executive had to learn that he could not just press a buzzer and delegate a task to a subordinate with confidence that it would be accomplished. Instead he usually found that he had to do the job himself by patient negotiation and reconciliation of opposing interests. In this respect I am sure the academicians had an advantage. They were usually more accustomed to doing things for themselves and seemed to have a surer instinct as to how such jobs must be handled in a huge bureaucracy.

The task of adjustment was particularly difficult for those businessmen who came to Washington relatively late in the game. For them the puzzle of following all the interwoven threads and of comprehending just how a huge lumbering machine like the WPB really functioned was little short of impossible. Two such men were Donald Davis and Walter Heller who were called to Washington by Eberstadt during the last weeks of

1942. Davis was then President of General Mills and Heller was head of a Chicago finance company that bore his name.

Although Donald Davis stayed for a long period with the War Production Board, he never seemed able to catch on as to what made the wheels go around. In this respect Walter Heller was the more astute of the two. He resigned and returned to Chicago after a brief stay of a few weeks. I remember vividly a talk I had with him just before his departure. He told me that he just could not make any sense out of the whole picture and felt that he had better get out before he made some unfortunate mistakes.

When thinking of academicians who were outstanding in their War Production Board performances, the names of three men come to mind. These were Lincoln Gordon, Bertrand Fox and William Y. Elliott. The first two were members of my staff in the Program Bureau, while Elliott was head of the Transportation Branch of the WPB. Gordon, then an assistant professor of Politics at Harvard, was brilliant in everything he did. In the later months of the year, long after my departure from the scene, he was made Program Vice-Chairman of the WPB. Since the war Gordon has served our government in a wide variety of important jobs, under Truman, Eisenhower, and Kennedy. At present he is United States Ambassador to Brazil.

Bertrand Fox, then an assistant professor of Statistics at Williams College, was the ablest and most brilliant statistician I have ever known. It was his task to analyze the requirements presented to us by the several claimant agencies. He had an uncanny ability to uncover subterfuges and padding in all these statements. Since the war he has covered himself with distinction in several different fields.

I did not have such a close association with William Elliott, who was and still is a professor of Politics at Harvard. I was always impressed, however, by the keenness of his intelligence and the breadth of his understanding. During the presidential campaign of 1960, Elliott served as a close advisor of Richard Nixon.

The
presidential
"must" programs

During my years in Washington I became convinced that Franklin Roosevelt had a positive genius for
creating confusion amongst his subordinates. It was the
President's practice to issue sweeping directives with an
apparent total lack of concern as to whether or not they
upset existing channels of authority or whether they ran
counter to earlier directives issued by him.

The calling of Charlie Wilson to Washington in order
to set him up as a counterweight to the influence of
Eberstadt in the War Production Board was described
in an earlier chapter. Also told was the story of how the
President deliberately upset the established lines of authority in the WPB in order to give Wilson something to

do, and thus created the inevitable conflict between Wilson and Eberstadt.

The President also called to Washington numerous business executives to take charge of different critical programs. Each was assured that nothing would be permitted to stand in the way of the accomplishment of the desired objective and was given a Presidential directive to this effect.

The executive would then undertake the job only to discover almost immediately the existence of previously issued directives of equal urgency to his own which ran directly across the path of his needs for critical materials and components. With one notable exception discussed later in this chapter, these individuals usually accepted the facts of life as they found them and did their best to get along with their assigned tasks in cooperation with other competing agencies.

This chapter discusses some further outstanding examples of the President's genius in creating confusion.

The aircraft program

During the months of December, 1941 and January, 1942, Winston Churchill spent several weeks at the White House reviewing with President Roosevelt every important aspect of the Allied war effort. Some time during Churchill's visit, the President suddenly announced to the world that the United States would produce 60,000 military aircraft in 1942, and 125,000 in 1943. Where the President obtained these staggering figures, and whether he issued the statement in order to impress Churchill, or to frighten the Germans and the Japanese, no one seemed to know.

Although actual aircraft production in 1942 fell far short of the Presidential program, Roosevelt refused obstinately to alter the much larger goal which he had announced for the succeeding year. During the early months of 1943 numerous unsuccessful efforts were made to convince the President that his aircraft objective was far removed from the realities of the situation. Roosevelt steadfastly refused to alter his announced goal of 125,000 planes and stated that if there were to be any change in the objective, it would be to revise it upward rather than downward.

The presidential "must" programs

At this time we were struggling to install an effective system of allocations and the President's attitude created a chaotic situation in the scheduling of aircraft production, and, therefore, in the whole system of making intelligent allocations. The difficulty arose from the fact that the main bottleneck was in the construction of airframes, while the production of aircraft engines and of most of the airborne equipment was maintained at the levels necessary to achieve the Presidential objective. Thus, we discovered, in the early spring of 1943, that total production of airframes for the full year would amount to not more than 95,000 units, even if training planes and gliders were included. This, of course, represented a magnificent achievement in itself even though it was far below the Presidential goal. One serious trouble was that aircraft engine production at the same time was running ahead of airframe production by some 33,-000 units.

Those directly concerned with the aircraft program were so overawed by the command from Mt. Olympus that they did not dare to tamper with the scheduling of aircraft production and related equipment. In fact, they were even unwilling to admit the possibility of failure of the Presidential program. Involved in this ridiculous situation were not only the top brass of the Air Force, but also numerous individuals in the WPB, such as the heads of the aluminum and aircraft branches. As a result, I was forced to listen to more double talk in this connection than I have ever heard on any other subject in my life.

Thus, at meetings of the Program Adjustment Committee, a standard pattern of dialogue developed between me, as chairman, and General Hopkins, the representative of the Air Force. On numerous occasions, the following exchange took place almost without the change of a single word:

General Hopkins—"Mr. Chairman, I wish to state for the record that the Air Force expects to complete the Presidential aircraft program exactly as planned. We will not agree to the slightest deviation from this objective."

Myself—"Mr. Secretary, have you recorded the General's remarks as requested? O.K.—Now, Hoppy, what do you really think?"

My query was always followed by a dead silence from General Hopkins.

The discrepancy between airframe construction and the production of engines finally became so glaring that Eberstadt felt compelled to take action. He instructed me to make a special trip to Wright Field, Dayton, Ohio, which was the headquarters for the Air Force procurement, in an effort to bring some order out of this mess. I left early one morning in a plane of the Air Transport Command, accompanied by Lincoln Gordon and Bertrand Fox.

Arriving at Wright Field about 10:00 A.M., we spent the next two hours with several Air Force officers, reviewing again and again the schedules of airframe and engine production. Despite all the efforts made to confuse us, we always emerged with the same conclusion: namely, that aircraft engine production was running ahead of airframe construction by total of some 33,000 units. Finally, since our hosts had been unable to convince us of the errors of our ways, we adjourned for lunch. It was understood that we would meet in the afternoon with the Commandant of Wright Field, Colonel Edwin W. Rawlings (now General Rawlings, Ret., and currently president of General Mills).

When we entered Rawling's office in the afternoon, the Colonel greeted us with a startling piece of news. He told us that the Joint Aircraft Committee (Air Force and Navy) has just completed a meeting in Washington about one hour earlier. At this session, the Committee had decided to change the delivery schedules of spare engines to be shipped overseas in the wake of the actual aircraft. Up to this point, most of the newly completed aircraft were flown directly to Africa or England, while the extra engines were shipped two months later on boats. The new decision, reached *by coincidence* on the day of our visit to Wright Field, was to fly the spare engines overseas concurrently with the aircraft for which they were intended.

As Colonel Rawlings summed up the matter neatly: "You see, Fennelly, this will advance the schedule of aircraft engine production by two full months and will eliminate 20,000 of the so-called excess of 33,000 units. What's the use of you and me arguing about an excess of 13,000 engines?"

Realizing that I was licked, I threw up my hands in disgust and asked the Colonel to have our plane alerted to fly us back to Washington. Later that evening we found ourselves stacked in heavy soup at 11,000 feet over the Washington airport. The plane was a twin-engine Lockheed. Suddenly, the plane's radio went out and great chunks of ice began to form on the wings and the cabin windows. Standing directly behind the pilots,

I watched the airspeed needle fall rapidly to the stalling speed of 125 m.p.h. All at once the pilot lowered the plane's nose, opened the engines to full throttle and high tailed it out to the west. We emerged in the clear over Wheeling, West Virginia, and finally put down at the Pittsburgh airport shortly after midnight.

Some time in May of 1943 the Presidential program of 125,000 aircraft was quietly abandoned. I never knew the identity of the courageous individual who finally convinced Roosevelt of the absurdity of the existing situation. In any event, order was quickly restored in the scheduling of the production of aircraft engines and airborne equipment. It was at this time that we suddenly discovered the existence of small surpluses in the supply of alloy steel and of magnesium.

The synthetic rubber program

When the Japanese invaded the Malayan Peninsula in December 1941, they created for the United States a crisis of the first magnitude in connection with the supply of rubber. In anticipation of such a contingency our government had stockpiled over half a million tons of crude rubber, but it was immediately recognized that such a supply was grossly inadequate for our wartime needs. The national economy of 1942 simply could not function unless the millions of passenger cars, trucks, busses, farm tractors, etc., could continue to roll on rubber tires. Also, it was clear that the war itself would be fought largely on the rubber tires for aircraft, trucks, jeeps, mobile artillery, etc.

Thus, our only path of salvation lay in the swift development from scratch of a synthetic rubber industry. The techniques of manufacturing artificial rubber from petroleum and other hydrocarbons had been evolved, largely in Germany, during the years just prior to World War II. Although considerable arguments existed at the time as to which type of synthetic rubber was best suited for various needs, the technical aspects of manufacture were well understood by our petroleum chemists and engineers. Nevertheless, the creation of such a huge new industry in the middle of a global war was a tremendous undertaking.

During more than a year after Pearl Harbor, while no effective system of allocations was in operation, the synthetic rubber program suffered from the general debasement of the currency of priority ratings. Finally, the lag in the construction schedules of the new rubber plants became so serious that drastic action had to be taken.

To break this bottleneck, President Roosevelt called to Washington William Jeffers, the president of Union Pacific Railroad. Jeffers was given one of the President's sweeping directives, stating that nothing was to stand in the way of the objective of speeding up the production of synthetic rubber. The new director of the Rubber Program was a short, stout man with a bull neck, and a voice to match. He had all the appearance and manner of one who would not brook any interference with his own planned course of action. For Jeffers, his directive had been engraved on a tablet of stone and brought down to him from Mt. Sinai. In his eyes every other directive which ran counter to his own was ipso facto fraudulent.

Shortly after Bill Jeffer's arrival at the War Production Board he was summoned to testify before the Senate Armed Services Committee, then under the chairmanship of Senator Harry S. Truman. I was requested by Donald Nelson to assist Jeffers in the preparation of a statement. When I volunteered my services, the Rubber Director made it clear that he did not need assistance from anyone. He would tell those Senators a thing or two about the rubber shortage and what he intended to do about it.

Nevertheless, I accompanied Bill Jeffers to the Senate Hearing Room and I listened spellbound while an extemporaneous statement, replete with four letter words, poured forth in a torrent from his lips. When he finished, the Senators applauded loudly, and, as a result of glowing press reports, Jeffers became something of a national hero overnight.

From that point on the Rubber Director was literally a bull in a china shop in his attempts to brush aside any opposition to his plans. Unfortunately, the rubber program was directly in conflict with the equally urgent program for expediting the production of aviation gasoline. Both required large amounts of equipment essential to the process of refining petroleum. To a lesser degree, the rubber program also ran foul of other urgent needs, such as the construction of landing craft.

I remember sitting in on a meeting called by Charlie Wilson, then executive vice-chairman of the WPB, in an effort to iron out some of these problems. Attending, in addition to several WPB officials like myself, were General Somervell and Admiral Robinson. After some fruitless discussion, Jeffers began pounding the table and shouted: "Gentlemen, if I can't get what I need for my program, I shall have no recourse but to go back home and tell the story to the American people."

After a moment of silence, General Somervell said quietly: "You know, Mr. Jeffers, I think you have a good point. Why don't we all go back and tell the people?"

Mr. Jeffers made no reply. It was the only time that any of us ever saw the old man stopped dead in his tracks with nothing to say.

Shortly thereafter, Cap Krug, then Program Vice-Chairman, instructed the Rubber Director to appear before the Program Adjustment Committee and give us a detailed statement of the requirements for his program. Bill Jeffers did not deign to appear in person but sent his deputy, Mr. Bradley, and several other members of his staff. *The presidential "must" programs*

For about two hours I did my best to elicit some coherent statement of requirements but finally had to abandon the attempt. Either these representatives did not understand the meaning of requirements, or else were determined not to give us the information. After obtaining a half-hearted promise from Bradley to submit a written statement of their requirements to the Program Bureau, I decided to terminate the session.

After looking around to make sure there were no females present, I then made the following statement:

"Gentlemen, since it is obvious that we are getting nowhere, I am about to adjourn this meeting. Before doing so, however, I am going to tell you about an incident that occurred at a meeting of the War Production Board in the early days of the war. The impending rubber shortage was very much in the minds of everyone, and the meeting was called to consider ways and means of curtailing non-essential uses of this material."

"Eventually the discussion got around to the subject of rubber contraceptives for males. At this point Leon Henderson is reported to have said that, as far as he personally was concerned, it would be all right to cut the length of this item in half, but he did hope that the total supply would not be reduced."

Finishing, I glanced at Admiral Williams on my left and saw that his face had turned beet red. I then realized there must be a woman in the room, seated directly behind me where I had not been able to see her. Stand-

ing up and looking straight ahead with a red face myself, I said: "Gentlemen, the meeting is adjourned."

To my amazement the young lady then came up to
me and made the following surprising statement:
"Please don't be embarrassed, Dr. Fennelly. I never understand stories; I only understand statistics."

I never learned her identity, but I must say that for a
female statistician, she was a remarkably good sport.

In retrospect I am inclined to believe that Bill Jeffers
was probably as good a choice as could have been made
at the time to take charge of the synthetic rubber program. Despite the disturbances that he created, Jeffers
did manage to bull through a substantial acceleration in
the nation's capacity to produce synthetic rubber. I certainly would not pretend to the wisdom of denying that
this service may not have been at least as great as the
damage which his activities caused to other urgent programs. The answer, of course, is that we did get the synthetic rubber that was badly needed, and we still managed to produce enough other equipment and supplies
to win the war.

The Manhattan Project

The Manhattan Engineer District, or simply the
Manhattan Project, was the code name used to desig-
nate the top secret program for the development of the
atomic bomb. In this particular area I have no possible
criticism of our wartime President. It must have taken
unusual courage and imagination on the part of Roosevelt to push ahead with this multi-billion dollar gamble
in the face of the profound skepticism of many of his
military advisors. Such a skeptical attitude was particularly evident in the case of Admiral Leahy, the
chairman of the Joint Chiefs of Staff.

In my opinion, the development of the atomic bomb by the United States in the middle of a global war was the most remarkable achievement of its kind in all military history. With nothing but the theories of physicists to go on, the whole task was accomplished in less than three years. How stupendous this undertaking was is made clear in Major General Leslie Grove's recent book: "Now It Can Be Told".

The presidential "must" programs

One of the most amazing aspects of the achievement was the whole-hearted collaboration attained amongst a host of theoretical scientists, engineers, business executives, and civilian and military representatives of our government. Another amazing aspect was the high degree of secrecy maintained in connection with the project during the entire period of development.

In order to be certain of having an ample supply of fissionable material, a two-pronged attack was made on this problem. A huge plant was erected at Oak Ridge, Tennessee, for the purpose of extracting the rare and highly fissionable element, U-235, from ordinary uranium, U-238. Another large industrial complex was created at Hanford, Washington, where ordinary uranium was converted into a new element, plutonium, by means of controlled fission reactions. The final link in the chain was created at Los Alamos, New Mexico. Here a large group of scientists and engineers was gathered, under the direction of Robert Oppenheimer, for the development of the actual mechanisms of the bomb itself. All of these vast operations had to be synchronized perfectly to be ready for the firing of the first test bomb in July, 1945.

The development of the atomic bomb by the Russians after the war pales in comparison with the American achievement. By this time the whole theory of atomic fission and the general techniques involved were well known to scientists throughout the world. Also, the Russians were working on a development already proven successful by the Americans. Finally, the Russians were helped enormously by Klaus Fuchs, the British scientist, who defected to the Communists, and probably by others as well.

My own contact with the Manhattan Project was slight and unimportant. One day in January, 1943, General Clay came to the War Production Board and asked to see Ferd Eberstadt and me alone. At this meeting he advised us he had been authorized by the Secretary of War to explain to the two of us what the Manhattan Project was all about. Because the War Department would be coming to the Requirements Committee with requests for large amounts of critical materials for this program, the Secretary felt it essential that someone in the WPB should understand the nature of the project. Clay's request, to which we readily agreed, was simply that these requirements be approved by us without discussion before our committees, or indeed with anyone else.

After Clay had told us the story of the atomic bomb development, my immediate, though unvoiced, reaction was: "My God, what an incredible waste of manpower and materials on a hare-brained plan that cannot work." I promptly put the whole subject out of my mind and never thought of it again until I read the news of the bomb exploding over Hiroshima. Consequently, no one could have been more surprised than I by this event.

Whenever I hear anyone bemoaning the immorality of the United States in its use of this frightful weapon, I think of the words of General Robert Eichelberger. As Commander of the Eighth Army, Eichelberger was scheduled to lead the attack on the main Japanese island of Honshu. After his return to the States in 1948, he said to me:

"Shortly after the occupation of Japan I spent considerable time examining the coastal defenses and intricate underwater obstacles erected in anticipation of our attack. As a result, I am certain we could never have brought Japan to her knees without at least one million American casualties. Every night, therefore, I thank the good Lord for the atomic bomb."

The presidential "must" programs

Relations with the military

I must re-emphasize here the point made in the Introduction that nothing in these pages is intended to reflect discredit upon our fighting forces in World War II. The epic story of valor shown by the men of our Army, Navy, Air Force and Marines in countless engagements shines forth like a beacon light for all to see. Certainly the words of a mere bureaucrat like myself, who fought the war in Washington, could neither add to nor detract from these magnificent achievements.

My story is the more prosaic one of relationships with members of the several services of supply. Here again I have nothing but admiration for most of these dedicated men who worked their hearts out at their tasks and suffered from the frustrations of being forced to remain in rear echelons instead of in the front lines of battle all over the world. In the succeeding pages are set forth some of the highlights of my associations with the leading individuals in each of these military agencies.

The Navy

During the first year of the War, our Navy suffered from something of an inferiority complex and, consequently, carried a large chip on its collective shoulder. Regular naval officers from admirals to ensigns were stung to the quick by the major disaster at Pearl Harbor, and by the lesser disaster eight months later at Savo Island. The Navy had always been aloof in its dealings with other agencies, but became unusually difficult to understand and cope with for many months after Pearl Harbor.

The official naval attitude was well exemplified in the personality of Admiral Ernest King, who was appointed Commander in Chief of the Navy after our entry into World War II. Tight-lipped and tough as a boot heel, King concentrated his attention solely on the problem of rebuilding the American Navy into a first-class fighting machine. Nothing was allowed to stand in the way of attaining this objective, and naval officers were apparently instructed to use any methods short of murder to obtain and hold the materials and equipment needed for their programs. The unbroken series of victories at sea by our Navy during the later years of the War provides convincing evidence of the success of King's leadership.

Amongst other things, Admiral King introduced a cult of extreme masculinity into the Navy. He would not permit any women inside the Headquarters Building of the Navy Department. Also, he was reported to regard any man as something less than a real man unless he had all the attributes of a brass monkey.

A characteristic story is told about King on the occasion of his first meeting with the Earl of Mountbatten. The latter was sent to the United States to take command of a British aircraft carrier which had undergone major repairs at the Norfolk Navy Yard after taking a frightful mauling from German dive bombers off the Island of Malta. When King and Mountbatten were introduced, the Admiral's only reported comment was: "And what, Sir, are your qualifications to be Commander of an aircraft carrier?"

My chief contacts with the Navy were Rear-Admiral Williams, the naval representative on the Requirements Committee, and his deputy, Captain Small. Williams was a kindly old gentleman who had been brought out of retirement to serve in Washington during the War. He functioned chiefly as a front for Jack Small, who was tough enough to measure up to the rigid standards of Ernie King.

An Annapolis graduate, Small had resigned from the Navy during the Thirties to enter business, but returned to the Service on the outbreak of war. He was a relentless and last-ditch fighter for every detail of the Navy's requirements presented to the Program Bureau. In addition, he proved himself to be a man of great personal bravery later in the War.

Jack Small had taken a leading part in the Navy's landing craft program. When D-Day in Europe was at hand, Jack sought for and obtained permission to test personally each of the several types of craft used in the Normandy landings. To make this test, he is reported to have undertaken five separate trips into and back from the beaches on D-Day, each in a different type of landing craft. I have never learned what decoration, if any, was awarded to Jack Small for this heroic achievement, but in my opinion, he should have been given the Congressional Medal of Honor.

As reported in an earlier chapter, my first run-in with the Navy was in connection with an effort to free up some Diesel locomotives for our domestic railroads. I was so astonished by the intransigeance of the naval officers with whom I dealt that I reported the matter to Jim Knowlson. The latter's comment was a classic Knowlsonism:

"Don't you realize, John, that until the Japs thrust those torpedoes into the arsenal of democracy, the Navy hadn't had a real fight on its hands since the battle of the Monitor and the Merrimac? Consequently, they have concentrated their efforts largely upon battling with the other services."

During the succeeding months I was confronted with numerous other instances of the Navy's stubborn resistance to any change in its programs. Amongst these were the appeal against the decree that prohibited the use of electric fans in their shore establishments and the bitter battle waged to include two heavily armored target ships and a huge floating drydock in their allocations. The culminating episode, however, was the Navy's reaction to the 20 percent cut ordered for all military requirements for the calendar year of 1943.

As previously reported, our study of military requirements as assembled under the Production Requirements Plan in the early fall of 1942 convinced everyone in the WPB that military demands for 1943 would be greatly in excess of our economy's ability to supply them. As a result, Donald Nelson in November, 1942, ordered a cutback of overall military requirements of 20 percent for the following year. It was clearly understood that the decree had reference to physical quantities of hardware to be produced in the calendar year. As the only available common denominator, however, the order was expressed in dollar terms—namely, as a cutback from $100 billion to $80 billion of hard goods.

When the revised military requirements for the first quarter of 1943 were presented to the Program Bureau, we discovered that the Navy alone amongst the services had failed to make any downward adjustment in its stated demands. After receiving numerous evasive answers from naval officials, Eberstadt felt compelled to bring the matter forcibly to the attention of Admiral Robinson, the chief of all naval procurement. After parrying repeated questions, the latter finally made the following bland admission: "Since the order was stated in dollar amounts we felt we would be meeting its terms by postponing payment on 20 percent of our requirements until the first quarter of 1944." Needless to say, the Navy requirements were promptly adjusted downward by the necessary 20 percent.

One more amusing anecdote of this kind is worth reporting. In the spring of 1943, the Planning Committee of the War Production Board became greatly concerned over the impending shortage of oil supplies at our west coast ports to meet the rapidly expanding demands of the war in the Pacific. Both crude oil reserves and refining capacities in this area were strictly limited, no pipelines were then in existence to bring oil and gasoline from the East, and our tanker capacity, in view of the heavy losses to German submarines, was barely sufficient to meet the needs of the conflict in Europe and Africa.

As possible means of alleviating the West Coast shortage, the Planning Committee decided to explore the possibility of a rapid development of the large Elk Hills Oil Reserve in Wyoming, owned by the Navy. Tom

Blaisdell, a member of the Committee, was commissioned to run the matter down. He promptly called on the Navy captain who had the Elk Hills Reserve under his jurisdiction. In response to Tom's question, the captain made a reply which should remain a classic for all military history: "You know, Blaisdell, we thought it would be a good idea to save that reserve for the next war."

The Army

Donald Nelson, in his book, *Arsenal of Democracy,*[*] complains constantly of the Army's efforts to dominate the national economy. One might almost conclude from reading Nelson's story that the nation was threatened by a coup d'état and a take-over by a military junta. Nothing, I am sure, could have been further from the truth.

When one considers the caliber of the men principally involved—Henry Stimson, Secretary of War; Robert Patterson, the Under Secretary; General Brehan H. Somervell, Chief of the Army Services of Supply; and his deputy, General Lucius D. Clay—the only possible conclusion is that the whole story was a myth fabricated by Nelson and his fellow New Dealers for their own political advantage.

Without exception these Army men were patriotic, high-minded Americans, and not one of them, I am sure, had any more ambition to dominate the national economy than I did myself. What they were anxious to do was to get on with the job of winning the war, and

---

*Nelson, Donald—*Arsenal of Democracy,* Harcourt, Brace & Company

111

they were fed up to the teeth with the inefficiencies and political shenanigans that were so prevalent in the War Production Board. It was this situation that led to a constant succession of rows between the Army leaders and the head of the WPB.

While I knew General Somervell, my contacts with him were limited and more or less casual. From all I could hear and observe, however, I am sure he was a strong, able soldier who had a tough job to do and would tolerate no nonsense in connection with the accomplishment of this objective. Of Somervell it could well be said that he did not suffer fools gladly.

My chief Army associations were with Somervell's deputy, General Clay, who was the Army representative on the Requirements Committee, and with Colonel James Boyd, who in turn was Clay's deputy.

Lucius Clay was (and is) a lean man of average size with hawk-like features. His deep-set, piercing eyes actually seemed to emit sparks when he was angry. Unquestionably Clay was the ablest military man I knew during the Second World War. An excellent administrator, a tough fighter for Army requirements, he was also that rare exception to be found in uniform—an officer with a broad statesmanlike outlook on the war as a whole. Thus, he was always ready to make concessions for demands of other agencies if he could be shown that the result would be beneficial to the overall war effort. My year of close association with Clay in Requirements Committee work is one of my happiest memories of the war.

That Lucius Clay's unusual talents were well recognized by others is shown by his later wartime and postwar record. In the summer of 1944 he was suddenly ordered to France to break up the log jam in the movement of supplies through the port of Cherbourg that had developed after the Normandy landings. About five months later he was called back to Washington to become deputy to Justice Byrnes in the Office of War Mobilization and Reconversion. Then in April, 1945, he was appointed Deputy Commander to Eisenhower of the American Army of Occupation in Germany. He then succeeded Eisenhower as Commander-in-Chief, with the rank of a four-star general, when the latter returned to Washington to become Chief of Staff of the Army.

Relations with the military

When I returned to my business in Chicago in the early winter of 1944-1945, I found my late senior partner, Charlie Glore, engaged in a running battle with Sewell Avery, the chairman of Montgomery Ward & Company. As a long-time director of Ward's Charlie had been trying to convince Avery that he should step aside in favor of a younger man, and was doing his utmost to find a properly qualified individual for the position.

In April, 1945, Glore happened to ask me if I had met anyone in Washington who might measure up to the job. Without hesitation, I told him that Clay was his man. He asked me to call Lucius on the phone and attempt to persuade him to come to Chicago to discuss the matter. When I reached Clay, he told me that he had just received the appointment to go to Germany and could not consider anything else at the time. Instead, he invited me to join him in his mission to Germany. Unfortunately, I was forced to decline.

After a brilliant record in Germany, which included the successful airlift to beleaguered Berlin, Clay retired from the Army. He was almost immediately appointed Chairman of the Continental Can Company, where he served with distinction for more than a decade. His latest service has been to act as President's Kennedy's personal representative in Berlin during the latest crisis in that city in 1962.

My last official contact with Clay was at the final meeting of the Requirements Committee that I attended before resigning from the WPB. On this occasion late in May of 1943 it was my job to present the proposed allocations for the third quarter of the year. There was one small item in the program which I knew would be displeasing to the Army. When I came to it in my presentation I turned to Clay and said: "Lucius, I know you won't like this item, but I am going to ask you to accept it as a final favor to me."

The General gulped hard and then replied: "All right, John, I shall accept it, but only as a favor to you."

Colonel James Boyd, Clay's deputy on the Requirements Committee, was a younger man by ten years, but also of outstanding ability. Born an Australian, Boyd had his early education in England, but completed his studies in the United States, where he finally acquired a Ph.D. in Geology. He became an American citizen and was a full colonel of the Engineers when I knew him in Washington. Highly intelligent, with great intellectual honesty, Jim Boyd was always a joy to work with.

Boyd spent eighteen months in Germany with General Clay and left there to become Dean of the Colorado School of Mines. Shortly thereafter he was appointed Director of the Bureau of Mines in Washington where he served for five years. Since then he has served as vice-president of the Kennecott Copper Company, and is now president of the Copper Range Company.

Of my many interesting experiences with the Army, two are highlighted in my memory. Both, by coincidence, involved relationships between our Army and the British. I learned at an early date that both Somervell and Clay were highly suspicious of the English.

They believed, with considerable justification, that our allies would resort to almost any tactics to obtain the supplies and equipment that they needed. If they were unable to secure their requirements through regular channels, they were always attempting to develop some new device by which they might be able to run around our Army's end.

One such device was the Combined Production and Resources Board. This body, at the suggestion of the British and with the approval of Donald Nelson, was created in the summer of 1942. It had the ostensible and logical objective of allocating materials and equipment between the British and American allies in accordance with strategic considerations. Donald Nelson became chairman and Sir Robert Sinclair, of the British Ministry of Supply, was named co-chairman.

Early in August of that year, Henry Aurand, a brilliant young brigadier-general of the International Division of the Army Services of Supply, was appointed executive director of the new organization. He was given offices in the War Production Board building and started to work at once.

The first official meeting of the Combined Board took place during the last week of August. It occurred while Jim Knowlson, my boss, was away on the fateful fishing trip from which he returned to discover he had been removed as Program Vice-Chairman of the WPB. In Knowlson's absence, I was invited to attend the session as Acting Chairman of the Requirements Committee.

When I entered the large conference room I found Nelson and Sinclair seated at the head of the table with several other WPB officials in attendance. In the background I noticed three Army colonels, none of whom I had ever seen before. I wondered immediately at the absence of both Sommervell and Clay.

115

General Aurand, the executive director, presented a report on a British proposal that 10,000 tons of armor-piercing shot steel be transferred from the September quota of the American Army to the British. Aurand concluded his report by recommending approval of the transfer.

Therewith Nelson spoke up: "The idea sounds all right to me—what do you think of it, Sir Robert?" Naturally, Sir Robert was in hearty agreement. Nelson then continued: "Well, in that case, we will recommend its approval to our American Requirements Committee."

Immediately smelling trouble for myself, I broke in: "Don, I am afraid I need a little clarification. Is this an order from you, as chairman of the War Production Board, to me? Or, shall I accept it as a recommendation on which you expect the Requirements Committee to take independent action?"

Coming from one in his position, Nelson's reply was a beauty: "Of course, we expect the Requirements Committee to take completely independent action."

The meeting broke up and I sat for a while alone at the table pondering what to do about the hot potato that had been tossed into my lap. Suddenly I felt a hand on my shoulder and saw Jean Monnet standing beside me. (M. Monnet was at that time a refugee from Occupied France, but later became internationally famous as the father of the European Coal, Iron and Steel Community).

The following exchange then ensued:

Monnet: "I hope you realize, young man, the tough spot you are in."

Myself: "I certainly do, Mr. Monnet, and I should like to ask you what you would do, if you were in my position."

Monnet: "I certainly should refuse to take action myself on the matter. Instead I should pass the buck back up to where it belongs, to the Chairman of the War Production Board."

Myself: "Thanks for the good advice. It will be followed—and promptly."

Early that same afternoon a previously scheduled meeting of the Requirements Committee was convened. I opened the session by reciting the story of the Combined Board meeting that morning. Before I could finish, Clay had risen halfway out of his chair in his wrath. I concluded quickly by adding:

"Please sit down, General; all I want to tell you is that I had nothing whatsoever to do with this affair. I shall refuse flatly to take any action in this connection and shall insist that the decision be made by the Chairman of the War Production Board."

Under the circumstances, Nelson had no alternative but to make a decision in line with his earlier recommendation.

The Army reaction was swift and dramatic. Henry Aurand disappeared almost immediately from the Washington scene, and reappeared shortly thereafter as a major-general in charge of the Sixth Service Command with headquarters in Chicago. A story went the rounds in Washington at the time that Aurand was called on the carpet by his commanding officer, General Somervell, and given the choice of staying in Washington as a major, which was his permanent rank at the time or of becoming a major-general in Chicago. Whether or not this story had any basis in fact, it is certainly correct that Henry Aurand was transferred to Chicago with the rank of major-general.

The Combined Production and Resources Board continued in being for some time thereafter, with Jim Knowlson succeeding Nelson as the American chairman. Since I never heard anything more of its activities, I can only conclude that it had handled itself with sufficient discretion to avoid running into difficulties with our Armed services.

The second incident occurred in April of 1943. One day the head of the Copper Branch of the WPB appeared at a meeting of the Program Adjustment Committee and requested a decision on an unusual matter. He advised us that the available supply of brass strip was insufficient to provide capacity operations for all the small-arms ammunition plants in Britain and the United States. He needed instructions as to which plants should be operated at full capacity and which should be left short of the necessary material.

Attempting to beat our military representatives to the punch, I broke in:

"Gentlemen, it seems clear to me that this problem involves strategic considerations, and is not one for the Requirements Committee to decide. I shall ask Don Nelson to request a decision in this matter from Admiral Leahy, Chairman of the Combined Chiefs of Staff. *

I then drafted an appropriate letter to Admiral Leahy for Donald Nelson's signature. When I presented it to Nelson, he complimented me profusely:

"You know, John, I wish everyone in our organization

---

*Admiral Leahy was chairman both of the Joint Chiefs of Staff and of the Combined Chiefs of Staff. The former consisted of the heads of the American Armed Services, while the latter consisted of representatives of the American, British, and Canadian military forces.

could handle things in such an orderly manner and through proper channels as you have done in this case. You will discover that we will receive a clearcut reply to this letter, and everything will be settled without any feathers being ruffled."

About ten days later, Colonel Boyd came into my office with a broad grin on his face. He said:

"The letter which you drafted from Nelson to Leahy has filtered down through the echelons of the Army and has finally reached General Clay's desk. Lucius suggested that I bring it over to you and together we draft an appropriate reply."

This we did with dispatch, requesting Nelson to divide the supply of brass strip pro rata amongst the American and British factories in accordance with their relative capacities. The draft letter then climbed back up the ladder of the Army hierarchy—from Clay to Somervell; from Somervell to General Marshall; from Marshall to Leahy—all with the necessary endorsements. Then Admiral Leahy signed the letter, unchanged, and it was delivered to the Chairman of the War Production Board.

About a week later I was called to Nelson's office, where he showed me the letter with great pride. His statement was:

"I told you, John, that by directing this problem through proper channels, we could expect an appropriate answer and solution. I can't tell you how pleased I am with this whole affair."

Somehow I managed to keep a straight face while listening to this pontifical statement. I certainly could not tell Nelson of the part I had played in this incident, because it might have destroyed some of his most cherished illusions.

Security regulations

I always had one simple philosophy with regard to military secrets. I realized that the less I knew about such matters the safer I would be from the risk of revealing something important by a careless slip of the tongue. Consequently, I never asked any questions and avoided as much as possible being privy to any knowledge that might be of aid and comfort to the enemy. I was confident that if my work required that I be given some such information, I would be so advised by the proper authorities. Such was the case in connection with the Manhattan Project. When I was told the story of this fantastic development, I did my best to put it completely out of my mind.

Any information which was deemed important to withhold from the enemy was known as classified material. To the best of my limited understanding, such material was divided into three categories: *Top Secret*, *Secret*, and *Confidential*. The first involved such matters of major strategic importance as the Manhattan Project, Overlord, the code name for the D-Day landings in Normandy, etc. The category *Secret* covered such items as troop and ship movements, the fighting strength of our military cadres, etc. *Confidential* was a catch-all classification that covered practically everything that was judged to be of any importance by the military authorities. Thus, a high percentage of the miscellaneous documents emanating from the War Production Board were automatically stamped *Confidential*.

Like most other wartime agencies, the WPB had its own Security Officer, whose job it was to police our practices with regard to the handling of classified material. I never knew of this individual's existence until he appeared in my office one day in August, 1942. It occurred when the Program Division was struggling to fight its way through the maze of statistical compilations that were overwhelming us in connection with the Production Requirements Plan.

The Security Officer waved in my face several sheets of statistical material, all stamped *Confidential,* which he had found scattered on the table of a deserted conference room. On his instructions I called all of our staff together, and we then listened to a lecture on the dangers to our nation if any of this material should fall into the hands of the enemy.

When he paused for breath, our friend was greeted by a spontaneous roar of laughter from all sides. Looking hurt and indignant he asked the meaning of this unseemly outburst. I am afraid that my explanation did little to improve his disposition. I said:

"You see, sir, none of us has been able to make any sense out of this mass of stuff. We had just been discussing the possibility of turning it all over to the Germans in the hope that they might be able to decipher it for us and let us know the answers. I do promise you, however, that we shall all be more careful in the future."

With that, the officer turned on his heel and left the room in a state of high dudgeon. I never saw him or heard of him again. I am glad to report, however, that these statistical compilations were no longer treated as classified material.

Public relations

The obverse side of security regulations was the information on the war's progress passed out to the public by our military authorities. I was always unhappy over the manner in which such information was handled. It seemed to me that the public relations officers of our

Armed Services were dominated by the Madison Avenue psychology of the advertising profession. Thus, unfavorable news was glossed over to a degree that was equivalent in many cases to falsehood, while favorable developments were greatly overstated. No one could complain of withholding information from the public in cases where the authorities had good reason to believe that the enemy was unaware of the real facts. What I objected to was the handing out of misinformation in instances where it was obvious that the enemy knew the entire truth. I always felt that the American people were capable of being treated like adults and would be more willing to make the necessary sacrifices if they knew all of the unpalatable facts.

A glaring case of this kind was the publicity treatment of the Pearl Harbor disaster. For many months thereafter all of Washington officialdom did its utmost to convince the American public that our losses had been of minor significance. At the same time, however, Japanese motion pictures were being run all over Latin America showing the frightful destruction and damge inflicted on our warships. Thus, the only people in the world who were kept in ignorance of the truth were the Americans. I am afraid that this situation was more the result of face-saving tactics on the part of the Administration than it was an unwillingness of military authorities to tell the unvarnished truth.

A similar situation arose in connection with our naval disaster at the battle of Savo Island in August, 1942. The official news releases from Washington gave the impression that our losses had been insignificant and that the engagement had been little more than a minor skirmish. Meanwhile, it was perfectly clear that the Japanese knew they had sunk four of our heavy cruisers (three American and one Australian) largely as a result of incredible ineptitude on the part of the Allied naval leadership. They also knew that they had thrown our entire naval operations in the South Pacific into disorder and thereby lengthened our campaign to conquer the Solomon Islands by several months.

The situation that really burned me up was our official handling of the news of merchant shipping losses caused by the German submarines. For a considerable period of time I was shown the monthly totals of actual allied shipping losses. These figures, of course, were secret. Almost concurrently I would read the published German claims of tonnage sunk during the preceding month. I was always astonished at the continued accuracy of these German reports. Frequently they were slightly larger but on some occasions they were actually smaller than our own official figures. Almost always the publication of the German figures was followed by a Washington news release stating that the Nazi claims were grossly exaggerated.

I remember particularly the figures for March, 1943, which represented the high watermark of success in the U-boat campaign. Our official figures revealed losses aggregating 586,000 tons of allied shipping, while the Germans claimed destruction of 595,000 tons, a difference of less than two percent. Shortly thereafter Frank Knox, the Secretary of the Navy, released a blast stating that our actual losses amounted to only a small fraction of the German claims. Obviously the Nazis knew what they had accomplished, and here again the American people were the only ones being fooled.

It was galling to me to realize that the United States, the seat of all righteousness, should be less scrupulous with the truth than the hated Nazis. Perhaps I was unduly idealistic in believing that any nation, in the midst of a major war, could be expected to have a strict regard

123

for the truth in reporting unfavorable developments. Thus, I am sure that, after the tide of warfare had turned heavily in our favor, our official reporting of events was much more accurate.

Relations with civilian agencies

Within a short time after Pearl Harbor, dozens of separate agencies had been created in Washington in an effort to provide representation for each important segment of our national economy. In addition to the many industry branches of the WPB, there were numerous agencies which had independent status, such as the Food Administration, the Maritime Commission, the Lend-Lease Administration, the Board of Economic Warfare, etc. This chapter presents some highlights of my associations with several of these groups. Also cov-

125

ered are my relations with members of the various British missions in wartime Washington.

The Maritime Commission

This agency might be classified either as a semi-military, or as a civilian body. Although it was administered by top-ranking naval officers, the Maritime Commission was not within the line of military command. Its task was to design, contract, finance and expedite the construction of the huge volume of merchant shipping which was essential to the winning of the war. Admiral Emory S. Land was chairman of the Commission and Admiral Howard Vickery served as Land's deputy. Willard Rockwell, the head of the Rockwell Manufacturing Company, was the top ranking civilian on the Commission and served as its representative on the Requirements Committee.

There can be no doubt that a highly efficient job was performed by the Maritime Commission. The immense tonnage of merchant shipping constructed in private shipyards under the direction of this agency was a vital factor in our winning of the war.

Although I did not know Admiral Land intimately, I had the greatest admiration for his abilities. A stocky little man, with a cheerful breezy personality, Jerry Land always seemed to know exactly what he wanted to do, and how he was going to do it.

I remember particularly an evening spent with Jerry Land at the home of the Henry Porters who were friends of ours from Chicago. As a member of the Office of Scientific Research and Development, Henry Porter was a key figure in the development of the proximity fuse. In addition to Admiral and Mrs. Land, my wife and I were the only guests on this occasion.

It happened to be the evening of the day on which Andrew Jackson Higgins, eccentric shipbuilder from New Orleans, had arrived in Washington with a great fanfare of publicity. In a press conference Higgins had announced that he had come to the capital to obtain a contract for 100 Victory ships, our latest standard model for merchant vessels. During cocktails, Jerry Land regaled us with the story of Higgins' visit at the offices of the Maritime Commission:

"When Higgins called on me this morning, I turned him over to Admiral Vickery and left the two of them alone all day. About five this afternoon I found the two men seated at opposite sides of a desk and glaring at each other like two tomcats on a backyard fence. It was obvious they had gotten nowhere in their negotiations. As a result, I broke in and said: 'Vick, why in the hell don't you give the old bastard an order for two ships and send him on his way?'"

"Immediately, Higgins' face lighted up like a lamp. He sprang to his feet and pumped my hand vigorously. It was clearly the first time anyone had spoken to him in language that he really understood."

My only other comment about the Maritime Commission involves a voluntary confession made to me by a member of the Commission staff shortly after my resignation from the War Production Board. This individual advised me that it was the regular practice of his agency to pad their requirements by an arbitrary twenty percent when they were presented to the Program Bureau. They did this in anticipation that approximately this amount would be cut off in the final allocations. I always suspected that similar tactics were employed by several of the other claimant agencies but the only concrete evidence I was ever able to obtain in this connection came from my friend in the Maritime Commission.

127

The Lend-Lease Administration

This agency was established by Act of Congress on March 11, 1941 in order to furnish munitions and other badly needed supplies to Britain, and later to Russia, in a manner which would obviate the need for cash payments. The name was clearly a euphemism for giving aid, first to our prospective allies, and later to our actual allies in World War II. The agency functioned under the leadership of Edward Stettinius, Jr., who, during the final months of the war, became Secretary of State. Averill Harriman served as deputy to Stettinius and ran the London office of Lend-Lease. H. C. L. Miller of Richmond, Virginia, was the Lend-Lease representative on the Requirements Committee.

The work of the agency was concentrated mainly upon aid to the British, because Harry Hopkins, from his post in the White House, insisted on maintaining personal supervision over all Lend-Lease grants to Russia.

The Lend-Lease Administration was staffed by a competent and dedicated group who, I am sure, did a thorough and efficient job, despite constant interference from the White House. The work with the British usually went ahead without serious difficulties, although as I have pointed out earlier, our English cousins were constantly engaged in devious schemes to obtain the supplies they wanted when they were not able to get them through the regular channels. The Russians presented a different kind of problem which is discussed a little later.

I was involved in one strange incident in connection with British Lend-Lease when the Program Adjustment Committee was brought into the problem of allocating lumber supplies. Somewhere in this discussion the subject of mahogany from British Honduras came up. To my amazement, I learned that the Lend-Lease Administration had been paying cash to the British Government for the raw lumber in Honduras, which was then shipped to the United States for processing into flooring for the decks of naval vessels. The finished product was then turned over free to the British. After expressing myself as being profoundly shocked at such an arrangement the subject was dropped. Later I learned that the Lend-Lease Administration had been so embarrassed by this revelation that they had forced the British to turn back all the cash paid to them for the mahogany lumber.

The Russians were always difficult to deal with. The main problem arose from the fact that the Soviet agents in this country had no authority of their own in handling requirements. All orders came direct from Moscow and the local representatives dared not deviate one whit from these demands, no matter how outrageous or ridiculous they might be.

For instance, I remember a request that came in from Moscow for alloy steel with the specification that it contain ten percent of nickel alloy. No one had ever heard of such a high percentage of nickel alloy in steel and the steel industry advised that it would not be possible to comply with the demand. Nevertheless, weeks of wrangling took place, with messages going back and forth steadily between Moscow and Washington, before the Russians were forced to accept a more normal mix of nickel alloy steel.

Another problem arose from the huge pile-up of supplies destined for Russia at our eastern seaports because of the lack of available shipping. At one time more than one million tons of steel products were rusting on the docks with no near-term prospect of moving them, and with the stockpile being added to constantly. Despite all our efforts to divert some part of this tonnage to other urgent needs, the Russians and Harry Hopkins refused steadfastly to permit this to happen. Eventually some part of these supplies was diverted but the larger part was shipped to Russia after the end of hostilities in Europe.

The culminating Russian incident with which I was involved occurred in the spring of 1943. At this time the Germans were retreating rapidly across Russia, tearing up railroad tracks as they withdrew. One day a group from the Lend-Lease agency appeared before the Program Adjustment Committee and presented an astounding request for 5,000 kilometres of automatic railway signal equipment for the Russian railroads.

At first everyone present was too dumbfounded to speak. Finally Colonel Boyd (Colonel James Boyd, the Army representative on the PAC) broke in: "Do you mind, Mr. Chairman, if I ask these gentlemen a few questions?" My approval was readily given and the following exchange took place:

Colonel Boyd: "How long will it take to manufacture this equipment?"

Lend-Lease Representative: "About two years.

Colonel Boyd: "And how long will it take to install after it is manufactured?"

Lend-Lease Representative: "Oh, about three years."

Colonel Boyd: "Good God, man, we will probably be fighting the bastards by that time."

Shortly after this dialogue the Lend-Lease group quietly folded their tents and withdrew from the meeting. Although we heard nothing more of this fantastic request, the incident did have one surprising sequel.

The following morning Jim Boyd called me on the phone to say: "I just wanted to make certain that no record of my remarks about the Russians was made in the minutes of yesterday's meeting."

After assuring him that he need have no worry in this connection, I asked the reason for his concern. Boyd then said:

"You won't believe it, John, but less than two hours after the meeting yesterday, I was called on the carpet by an Assistant Secretary of State and taken to task for my remarks about our Russian allies. I replied that since this was a secret meeting I felt I had the right to say exactly what I thought. It is disconcerting, however, to realize how quickly such information gets into the hands of the New Deal Gestapo."

The office of Civilian Supply

This agency was established to take care of the general needs of the civilian sector of the economy not covered by other special agencies, such as the Office of War Transportation, the Petroleum Administration for War, etc. At the outset it was headed by Leon Henderson who, a short time later, was made director of the OPA, or Office of Price Administration. At this point the direction of Civilian Supply was turned over to Joseph Weiner, a hard-boiled New Deal lawyer from Philadelphia.

I had nothing but respect for Joe Weiner. He ran a taut and efficient ship and stood for no nonsense. Very properly he conceived his task not as one of obtaining the maximum possible of strategic materials for civilian use but only the minimum which he regarded as essential to maintain the efficient operation of our productive machine.

I had a few run-ins with Joe Weiner but for a long

time I thought that our relations were on a mutually friendly basis. I was rudely shocked out of this frame of mind by an incident that occurred in the early spring of 1943. At this time my boss, Ferd Eberstadt suggested that I take a trip to Canada to study the Canadian techniques of handling allocations. He also suggested that I take with me a military and a naval aide.

Naturally I was delighted with the whole idea, and promptly selected Colonel James Boyd as my military aide, and Commander Henry S. Morgan as my naval aide. Shortly before our departure Eberstadt had a visit from Joe Weiner. Ferd was advised by Weiner that I must be anti-Semitic, because of my failure to include in my party a representative of the Office of Civilian Supply. When Eberstadt told me of this, my only reply was that the charge was so absurd that I refused to take notice of it, and certainly I saw no reason to include a representative of Weiner's agency.

Our four-day trip to Canada, under the aegis of Jock Carswell, the Canadian Deputy Minister of Supply in Washington, was thoroughly delightful. I am afraid, however, that we spent more time in being wined and dined by our Canadian hosts than we did in a serious study of the Canadian system of allocations.

My principal friend in the Office of Civilian Supply was Maurice Wertheim. As deputy to Joe Weiner, Wertheim served as this agency's representative on the Program Adjustment Committee. Maurice was one of the most attractive and cultured gentlemen I have ever known. A graduate of Harvard, he had amassed a large fortune as the head of a New York investment banking firm which bore his own name. In addition, the wide range of his interests was extraordinary. He owned one of the finest collections of French Impressionist paintings in the United States. Also, he was an excellent play-

132

er of chess and bridge, a first-rate fly-fisherman, and an expert with a shotgun.

I had the good fortune to spend one weekend with Maurice shooting ducks and pheasant on his magnificent preserve at Great South Bay on Long Island. I also had the luck to spend two evenings at his beautiful home on Massachusetts Avenue playing bridge with him and Charles Goren. Finally, when I resigned from the War Production Board, a farewell party was given for me by Maurice on the lawn of his home. The unexpected death of Maurice Wertheim a few years after the end of World War II was a real blow to me, as I am sure it was to his many other good friends.

The British

Because of the importance of their relations with the United States, the British Government saw to it that all of their representatives in Washington were a hand-picked lot. I had the good fortune to know a considerable number of these attractive individuals, and my associations with them form one of the most pleasant memories of my wartime experiences.

I had two pre-war friends of long standing on the staff of the British embassy. The first of these was Colonel Rex Benson, British military attaché. In civilian life Rex was head of a prominent private banking firm in London known as Robert Benson & Co. In pre-World War I days, my late senior partner, Marshall Field III and Benson had attended Eton together. Starting with this friendship our two investment firms had enjoyed many years of mutually pleasant and satisfactory business relations.

Rex Benson was, and still is, one of the most attractive and distinguished Englishmen I have ever known.

His wife is a lovely American, whose parental home was in Lake Forest, Illinois, where I have resided for more than twenty-five years. Now Sir Rex Benson, my friend has retired from active business and spends a large part of his time on a beautiful farm in Sussex.

My other old friend was Noel Hall, British Minister of Economic Warfare. Hall and I had studied economics together at the Princeton Graduate School in the Twenties when he came to the United States as a Commonwealth Fellow from Oxford. Noel even spent one Christmas vacation with me at my parents' home in Kansas City. Two more different personalities than Noel Hall and Rex Benson one could not imagine; Hall being completely a scholar and academician, while Benson was every inch man of the world. Nevertheless, both of them were later knighted by their Queen for outstanding accomplishments in their own respective fields of endeavor.

When war broke out in Europe in 1939, Great Britain promptly sent one of her most distinguished sons, Lord Lothian, to become the British Ambassador to the United States. Born Philip Kerr, Lothian was a member of the Howard family whose patents of nobility antedated the Protestant Reformation in England. Consequently, the Howards, like the Percys, had retained their Roman Catholic faith.

In this respect, however, Lothian was a maverick, because he had deserted the Catholic Church to become a Christian Scientist. It was said that this change was the result of his life-long devotion to Nancy Langhorne of Virginia, who later became the famous Lady Astor, and was herself an ardent Christian Scientist. In any event, Lord Lothian did join the Christian Science Church, and also remained a bachelor all his life.

134

As Philip Kerr, Lothian had served as Lloyd George's private secretary during the later years of World War I, and accompanied the British Prime Minister to the Versailles Peace Conference. Here he met and established a life-long friendship with my late father-in-law, Norman Davis.

I first met Lothian at the Davis home in Alexandria, Virginia, early in December, 1939. I had come to Washington to attend a dinner of the Gridiron Club and spent the weekend with the Davises. As a result, I was present at a luncheon which they gave on Sunday. Amongst the guests were Lord Lothian, and Rear-Admiral Harvey Ellis of the United States Navy. Ellis at the time was the officer in charge of patrolling the so-called Neutrality Belt which President Roosevelt by decree had established along the Atlantic Coasts of both North and South America.

After luncheon when the men were drinking coffee alone, I turned to the Admiral and said: "Sir, I should like to ask you some dumb questions about the German pocket battleships. The papers have been so full of them recently that it would be very interesting if you would tell us what you really think of their fighting qualities." (At that time at least two of the three pocket battleships—the Deutschland, the Admiral Scheer, and the Graf Spee—were known to be on the high seas and engaged in raiding allied shipping.)

The Admiral's reply was prompt: "I'm glad you asked that question because it happens to be a personal hobby of mine. I really believe these vessels are the most overrated warships afloat. They have neither the armor to stand up to a real battleship, nor the speed to run with a cruiser. I should love to take one of them on with two of my heavy cruisers. I'd even be willing to take on one with a single heavy cruiser. She would probably get me, but I would guarantee to put her in such shape that she would be a sitting duck for the next gunboat that came along."

At this point Lothian broke in: "Admiral, it is now my turn to ask a dumb question. What would happen if one of your patrolling warships should encounter the Admiral Scheer off the coast of Brazil?"

Admiral Ellis answered quickly: "Well, you see, Sir, we are not actually at war with Germany. We would merely exchange recognition signals. You must realize, however, that it is my duty to report to Washington the location of any belligerent warships found in the neutrality zone. I can assure you, Sir, that her location would be reported in a code that the British Navy would have no trouble in breaking down."

I was thrilled by this conversation, including as it did an insight into naval warfare and an unusual exchange of international amenities between the British and ourselves. The next afternoon (Monday) found me in the New York office of my firm, where I promptly reported the story to one of my partners, Wright Duryea.

My partner looked at me silently for a moment and then said: "Apparently, John, you haven't seen the afternoon papers. They are full of a battle that has just taken place off the coast of South America between a German Pocket battleship and three British cruisers."

Later when I had learned the full story of the battle of the River Plate, I was struck by three unusual facts:

1. That the battle had occurred only a few hours after our conversation in Washington.

2. The amazing accuracy of the estimate by Admiral Ellis of the fighting qualities of the pocket battleships. The Graf Spee had put the heavy cruiser Exeter out of action, but the latter, together with the light cruisers, Ajax and Achilles, had so damaged the Spee that she

was forced to seek her own self-destruction in the harbor of Montevideo a few days later.

3. That Lord Lothian had known exactly what he was talking about when he referred to the Admiral Scheer off the coast of Brazil. Some days earlier a pocket battleship had been sighted off the west coast of Africa which the British Navy had been advised was the Admiral Scheer rather than the Graf Spee. This vessel had steamed full speed to the west, and the three British cruisers had been planted off the coast of Brazil to intercept her.

Somewhat accidentally I obtained an interesting sidelight on Lord Lothian in the spring of 1940. Some time in May of that year I made a brief trip to Washington on business and returned to Chicago by air. On the plane I found myself next to a Catholic priest who turned out to be the Most Reverend James H. Ryan, Catholic Bishop of Omaha. We promptly engaged in conversation which continued without interruption for the four hours of our slow flight. Bishop Ryan was one of those highly sophisticated, intelligent Catholic priests than whom there are no more interesting people in the world to meet.

He told me that he had just completed a week's visit to the Catholic Apostolic Delegation in Washington. He then explained in some detail the work of the staff of that office in their efforts to maintain close and cordial relations with all of the embassies in Washington. The bishop admitted, however, that they had never been able to get anywhere with the British embassy because of the religious beliefs of that nation's ambassador.

When I confessed to an acquaintance with Lord Lothian, Ryan was eager to have me tell him everything I could about the ambassador. He finally added somewhat ruefully: "You know, Mr. Fennelly, we Catholics can understand how one might leave our church to become an Episcopalian or a Presbyterian but it is completely incomprehensible to us that anyone could abandon Catholicism to become a Christian Scientist."

Lord Lothian's life ended tragically only a few months after this unusual discussion, when he suffered a ruptured appendix. Steadfastly refusing to undergo surgery because of his religion, he contracted peritonitis and died within a week at the British embassy. Lord Lothian was then succeeded by Lord Halifax as British ambassador to Washington.

Another outstanding and attractive Englishman with whom I had a casual acquaintance in Washington was Field Marshall Sir John Dill, who became Chief of the Imperial General Staff shortly before the big German offensive in May of 1940. He remained in this post until right after Pearl Harbor when he was succeeded as C.I.G.S. by Sir Alan Brooke. Dill then accompanied Winston Churchill to Washington where he served as the British member of the Combined Chiefs of Staff. Later during the war he died at his post in Washington and, at the request of Lady Dill, was buried in United States Military Cemetery at Arlington, Virginia.

I first met Sir John Dill at a dinner party in January, 1942. It was during the period when Winston Churchill was making his prolonged visit at the White House. During dinner Dill regaled the group with one of the most delightful anecdotes that I heard during my years in Washington.

"For more than twenty-five years," began Dill, "I have had as a batman (orderly) a sergeant of the Royal Marines. The sergeant came to me last Saturday and said: 'You know, Sir John, I have never laid eyes on the P.M. Couldn't you possibly fix it so that I could catch a glimpse of him while he is here in Washington?'"

"I told the sergeant that this would be easy for me to arrange; that next morning I would give him a message to the Prime Minister with instructions on the envelope that the bearer deliver it personally into the hands of Churchill."

"The following morning (Sunday) the sergeant presented himself at the White House with the message. He was escorted by a guard to the elevator on the first floor and told to press the button for the second floor. Unaccompanied he ascended and soon found himself at the head of a long corridor with no one else in sight. He was standing there wondering what to do when a door suddenly opened and out came President Roosevelt in his wheel chair."

"Good Lord, man," said Roosevelt, "What in the world are you doing here?" When the sergeant had explained his mission, the President said: 'Follow me,' and trundled his chair rapidly down the corridor."

"When they arrived at the door of Churchill's bedroom, which happened to be the Lincoln room, the President raised his good leg and kicked the door open. Peering in, the two men saw Churchill, stark naked, pacing across the floor apparently lost in thought, and with a huge cigar firmly clenched in his teeth. All I can say is that the sergeant really saw the P.M."

Lean, handsome, and straight as a ramrod, Sir John Dill was every inch a professional soldier; and, on the occasions when I saw him, he was the soul of courtesy. He was, in fact, the beau ideal, in appearance and bearing, of what I thought a British field marshal should be.

— — — — —

Sometime in the fall of 1942 my secretary came into my office in the War Production Board and announced: "Mr. Fennelly, there's a Mr. Fennelly outside to see you."

139

"Is it my brother?" I inquired.

"No, it is not Commander Fennelly; it is a man I have never seen before."

"For heaven's sake, bring him in; I have never seen another one myself."

There then entered a tall, blond Englishman who, in a perfect Oxonian accent, introduced himself as Reginald Fennelly. I learned that he was a permanent official of the British Foreign Office and was then serving in the British Embassy. I learned later that he was the top-ranking member of the embassy staff, junior only to Sir Ronald Campbell and Noel Hall, both of whom had ministerial rank.

My namesake then told me that he had seen my name and decided it would be interesting for us to become acquainted. I was delighted, and for the next hour we sat and chatted about our respective backgrounds and careers. I learned that his grandfather, like my own, had been born in Dublin and moved to London as a young man, where both of our fathers were born. As a result, we decided that we must be some kind of distant cousins.

I never saw Reginald Fennelly again, although our meeting was an exceedingly pleasant one. He was a few years older than I, and was what I would describe as a perfect example of the old School Tie Englishman. A few years ago I heard that on retirement from the Foreign Office, he had been made Sir Reginald Fennelly.

About a month after our meeting there occurred an extraordinary coincidence which involved my namesake. One morning I noticed in the In-Coming box on my desk a strange looking sheaf of papers. (Every bureaucrat has an In-Coming and an Out-Going box on his desk, and one of the chief objectives of bureaucratic life is to shift papers from the In-Coming to the Out-Going box as rapidly as possible.)

Picking up the bundle I noticed a covering note on a small memorandum pad which read as follows:

From the Ambassador's Desk

To:

> Sir Ronald Campbell
>
> Mr. Hall
>
> Mr. Fennelly

Glancing through the documents I realized immediately that they were copies of a week's exchange of confidential cables between Anthony Eden, the British Foreign Secretary, and Lord Halifax. These papers, routed through the top echelon of the embassy staff, apparently never reached Reginald Fennelly. Instead, in some inexplicable manner, they had been taken out of the embassy, carried clear across Washington to the Social Security Building and deposited on my desk.

Having become convinced by a casual perusal of the cables that there was nothing of particular interest to me, I called my friend, Noel Hall, at the British Embassy, and said:

"Noel, I'm sure you won't believe me, but I have here on my desk a week's exchange of cables between Anthony Eden and Lord Halifax. I am astonished because I always thought you British were so meticulous about security matters. I haven't the vaguest idea how they got here, but if you will send a messenger to my office, I shall deliver them into his hands."

The papers were returned, and I learned later that all hell then broke loose in the British Embassy. No one ever troubled, however, to tell me whether or not they were able to find out how this strange miscarriage had taken place.

An
appraisal
of
F.D.R.

Chapter xiv

Perhaps it is presumptuous of one who had no personal relations with President Roosevelt to attempt to pass judgment upon our wartime leader. Nevertheless, no one could spend almost three years in Washington during the war without acquiring some definite opinions regarding this extraordinary individual. In the following paragraphs I have attempted to set forth a kind of balance sheet, listing first the virtues, or asset side of the Roosevelt character; and, second, his shortcomings or liabilities. This discussion is limited to an appraisal of Roosevelt as a wartime leader of our Nation, and no attempt is made to pass judgment upon his pre-war career.

Assets:

No one can doubt that Roosevelt possessed dynamic qualities of leadership. Despite his physical infirmity, he had an exuberant vitality, a magnificent speaking voice, and a most engaging personality. All of these combined to make him a natural leader of men.

He had also ample courage to carry through to any objective on which he had set his mind. I have already written of his courage in carrying out the multi-billion dollar gamble for the atom bomb. Perhaps this was a gambler's recklessness, but it did pay off, and it was the kind of courage out of which great leaders are made.

His choice of military leaders for the Second World War was magnificent. In Generals Marshall, Mac-Arthur, and Eisenhower he had a team of Army leaders that was extraordinary. I have never known anyone close to George Marshall who did not believe that he was one of the great men of our time. Certainly Douglas MacArthur will go down in history as one of the greatest military geniuses of the Twentieth Century.* Although Dwight Eisenhower did not have the rare military talents of his counterpart in the Pacific, he did possess organizational and diplomatic abilities of a high order, and it was these qualities which were particularly needed to lead the successful allied war effort in Africa and Europe.

For the Navy, Roosevelt's selections were equally outstanding. In Admirals King and Nimitz he had two

---

*In the early spring of 1945, when the war in Europe was drawing to a close, the British sent a military mission headed by one of their top generals on a tour of the Pacific Theatre to determine what contribution, if any, Great Britain might make in this battle area. In the preamble of his report, this British General declared that not only had MacArthur made no mistakes, but that his entire campaign in moving north across the Pacific was in conception and execution one of the most brilliant in all military history.

unusually strong and able men. Ernest King and Chester Nimitz by the force of their personalities succeeded in converting our Navy from a snug, over-confident organization at the war's outset into the finest fighting machine that ever sailed the seas.

Moreover, the President gave loyal support to his military commanders throughout the war. As far as I know, he also accepted their advice, at least insofar as matters of a strictly military character were concerned.

We turn now to the liability side of the Rooseveltian balance sheet.

In contrast to his brilliant record of leadership in the direct military aspects of the war, Roosevelt is subject to serious criticism for his handling of the civilian sector of our wartime economy. It has always seemed to me that the President was thoroughly bored with the problems of the home front. Instead, his mind appeared to focus instinctively upon the grand strategy of the war and upon our far-flung battle fronts. As a result, he seemed resentful of being required to turn his attention to the more prosaic questions relating to the production of the sinews of war in the United States.

Such a frame of mind would account for the slapdash manner with which Roosevelt issued sweeping directives that were frequently in conflict with those which he had issued previously. It would also account for his creation of, and rigid adherence to unrealistic production goals, such as the aircraft program already described in detail. Finally, it would help to account for some of his unfortunate appointments, which were largely political in nature, such as Donald Nelson as chairman of the War Production Board and Leon Henderson as head of the Office of Price Administration.

On the other hand, it must be admitted that Roosevelt succeeded in gathering around him a large group of outstanding civilians. To mention just a few of this large group of fine, patriotic men I would cite Henry Stimson, Secretary of War, Robert Patterson, his Under Secretary, John McCloy, Assistant Secretary of War, and Robert Lovett, Assistant Secretary of War for Air. In the Navy Department mention should be made of James Forrestal, Under Secretary, Ralph Bard, Assistant Secretary, and Lewis Strauss, a civilian who became a rear-admiral.

Roosevelt realized even before the outbreak of hostilities that he would need the assistance of a large number of business executives. Having induced these men to come to Washington, the President was fortunate that the high sense of patriotism of most of these individuals induced them to accept without complaint the cavalier treatment which they received from the occupant of the White House. First, he kept everyone in a constant state of confusion by his issuance of conflicting directives. Second, he made no apparent attempt to check the unceasing harassment of business executives by the New Deal Palace Guard. It would seem obvious that, in the midst of a global war, the Chief Executive could be expected to call a halt to all such political infighting. Finally, he was not above deliberately double-crossing some of these men, as in the case of Ferdinand Eberstadt, when it was politically expedient for him to do so.

Next, I am convinced that Roosevelt, during World War II became a victim of the disease described by Lord Acton, the famous British historian: "All power corrupts, and absolute power corrupts absolutely."

By the time Roosevelt was elected President for his third term in 1940, I believe that he felt himself above and beyond the rules of conduct that apply in the case of ordinary mortals. His megalomania had reached a point where he felt himself master of all that he surveyed. He had achieved such confidence in his own wisdom that he felt justified in using almost any means to reach his objectives.

The symptoms of this disease were revealed by the methods which Roosevelt employed in deliberately leading our country into war while promising at the same time to keep us out. After the fall of France in 1940, it became clear to all competent observers that the President had plotted a course for the United States that could only lead to direct intervention. Meanwhile, however, he continued to reassure the American people with such phrases as: "I say to you again and again that never will your sons be called upon to fight in a foreign war." Such conduct can only be described in terms of supreme arrogance and double-dealing.

These symptoms were also evident when he made sacrificial goats of Admiral Kimmel and General Short after the Pearl Harbor disaster. According to Kimmel's book on the subject, these two men were never advised of the breaking of the Japanese code and were kept in the dark with regard to most of the vital information on Japanese activities which was available to the top echelons in Washington. As stated earlier, I cannot subscribe to the theory that Roosevelt deliberately planned Pearl Harbor. It is equally clear to me, however, that the blame for this catastrophic surprise can only be placed at the door of the President and of his top military advisers. In attempting to shift this guilt to the local commanders in Hawaii he was playing politics of a very low order.

As the war progressed, the President's judgment in matters of national policy deteriorated steadily while his sublime faith in his own wisdom continued to grow. Such was clearly evident in his decision to demand the unconditional surrender of Germany. While the vindictive Morgenthau plan to convert postwar Germany into a simple agrarian economy was never officially adopted by the American Government, the basic idea behind this plan of destroying Germany seemed to be inherent in the President's policy of unconditional surrender.

Doubtless such a decision was a wise one in the case of our own Civil War, but as a policy for the Second World War in Europe it was sheer insanity. It did not require any great prescience at the time to realize that this program was almost certain to deliver central Europe into the hands of Soviet Russia.

Winston Churchill foresaw this danger when he advocated an attack through the Balkans which he described as "the soft under-belly of Europe". His plan was vetoed by the American military command solely on the basis of strategic considerations. In this they were probably correct, but Churchill's plan did make sense as a means of keeping the Russians out of central Europe.

The American Government then steadfastly refused to listen to the German pleas to be allowed to surrender to the Western Allies. I am convinced that, if we had been willing to accept this surrender, the war in Europe would have ended many months earlier, and the Russians would have been stopped at their pre-war frontiers.

When Germany attacked Russia in 1941 my fondest hope was that these two military powers would succeed in destroying one another. In fact, I was heartily in sympathy with the idea I heard expressed by a Polish colonel at a Washington dinner in the spring of 1943. The colonel's statement went as follows:

"You know what is the greatest ambition of my life. It is to be in Berlin and watch the last Russian kill the last

147

German. Then I myself would have the supreme pleasure of killing the last Russian."

Unfortunately, the last Russian was not killed, and, largely as a result of the American policy of unconditional surrender, Soviet Russia was left in a position to plague the international relations of western Europe and the United States for the indefinite future.

No one should blame the American military leaders for this situation. In the finest tradition of our armed services, they conceived their task solely as one of destroying the enemy and not as one of making national policies. The blame, therefore, lies squarely on the shoulders of Franklin Roosevelt and on no one else.

Nowhere was Roosevelt's megalomania seen more clearly than in his dealings with the Russians. Apparently the President was convinced that he was the chosen instrument of the Lord to lead Russia back into the family of civilized nations after the war's end. He even believed he could make a Christian out of "Good Old Uncle Joe" Stalin. How else can one explain his constant solicitude for Russian feelings, and the many vital but unnecessary concessions which he made to them at Teheran and Yalta? It is almost too bad that Roosevelt did not live to hear the revelations about Stalin which were made after his death by the succeeding gang in the Kremlin.

A revealing little story regarding the arrogance of Roosevelt and his family was told to me by Norman Davis. When the Pacific War was at its grimmest, Mrs. Roosevelt decided to make a tour of the Pacific battle areas to boost the morale of our fighting forces. As an appropriate costume for the trip, she had tailored for herself a uniform of the American Red Cross. The fact that she had absolutely no right to wear this uniform did not seem to bother Mrs. Roosevelt in the slightest.

148

When the ladies of the American Red Cross learned of this, their indignation knew no bounds. They went to their chairman, Norman Davis, and demanded that he lodge a personal protest with the President. When Mr. Davis complied with this demand, Roosevelt looked up with a bland smile and said: "Norman, don't you think it is worth it to get her out of the country for a few months, no matter what kind of a uniform she wears?"

An appraisal of F.D.R.

At this point it should be clear that, as far as I am concerned, there was no balance in the Roosevelt balance sheet; the liabilities were far in excess of the assets. And I cannot believe that he will be judged differently in the long perspective of history. Unlike Lincoln, the shadow of Roosevelt does not seem to be lengthening with the passage of time. In fact, there are already signs that it has begun to shrink back to that of a consummate politician who brought little of lasting good to his people.

Yet I cannot share the feelings of many of my fellow countrymen who look back on Franklin Roosevelt as the devil incarnate. As an extreme example of this view, a paragraph from the last will and testament of a man named Herbert Champlin is worth citing. Champlin was a rugged individualistic businessman of the old school. By his own efforts he built a large oil empire in Oklahoma. When he died some time around the end of World War II, he included in his will the following gratuitous remarks about Roosevelt:

"I am arriving toward the end of a pretty long and busy life, filled with the usual amount of happiness and sorrow. I have no ill feeling toward anyone, except to be truthful I must mention President Roosevelt, and I hope no one feels ill toward me."

In my book, Roosevelt was an extraordinarily able politician who possessed unique talents for leadership.

As I see it, he had all the qualities to make a great statesman except for an overweening sense of his own importance on the one hand, and a lack of intellectual integrity on the other.

Memoirs
of a
bureaucrat

Life in
wartime
Washington

At one time or another during the war, at least so it seemed to me, practically everyone I had ever known spent some time in Washington—officers and civilians en route to overseas billets, and those returning home to report, or for reassignment—business executives by the thousands who journeyed to the Capital to straighten out their problems of handling military production under governmental control. All of these transients gave the city an atmosphere of hectic gaiety and of a never-ending college reunion in the midst of a global war.

Fortunately, or unfortunately, I had neither the time nor the financial resources to become involved in the Washington cocktail circuit. Working ten to twelve hours a day for six or more days a week on a small government salary left me little opportunity for such extra-curricular activities. Nevertheless, I never looked down my nose at those who were able to participate. There was something very poignant in the brief gaiety of the men about to leave to risk or lose their lives in far-off battle areas; as well as those who had just returned from such grim scenes.

I was very fortunate to rent an attractive home for my family in the Chevy Chase, Maryland, section of metropolitan Washington. A well built, two-story brick house, with three bedrooms and two baths, as well as a maid's room and bath, provided ample space for my wife and myself, three small children, a nurse and a cook. The establishment had an ample front lawn and a two-car garage in the rear to house the two Studebakers that we had brought on from Chicago. All of this cost me throughout the war the large rental of $125 per month.

Looking backward from the present high level of living costs, I find it hard to believe how comfortably we lived on my small government salary which was our only source of income. This salary was fixed at $700 per month when I first joined the WPB, and rose by gradual stages to the munificent sum of $900 when I was made Director of the Program Bureau. Yet somehow I was never aware of any real financial stringency, despite the necessity of supporting a family of five, along with two excellent servants. I even managed to save enough to purchase $1,500 in War Bonds during my first two years in Washington. The only times I worried about finances were during my numerous airplane trips. On such occasions I couldn't avoid concern as to what might happen to my young family if I should be bumped off.

We all had plenty to eat, although the fare was far from elaborate. The three children attended an excellent nearby public school, and we had little occasion to spend money on clubs, entertainment or travel. I do recall that the shortage of fuel oil forced us to maintain the house temperature at 55 degrees on winter nights but this was probably healthy for all of us.

I rode to and from work in a car pool with my friends, Linc Gordon, Bert Fox, and Blackie Smith. My exercise consisted chiefly of mowing the lawn, washing the cars, and helping the children with small Victory garden on Sundays. Yet, except for a recurring sinus infection, I managed to stay in excellent health throughout the war.

Our chief alcoholic stimulant was Cuban gin which tasted something like hair oil. Nevertheless, it seemed palatable enough to those of us whose stomachs had become zinc-lined as a result of living through all the years of Prohibition. I shall never forget my joy at receiving as a present on Christmas of 1942 a case of Booth's House of Lords gin. It was given to me by my college roommate, Jim Douglas, who was then serving as Deputy Chief of Staff of the Air Transport Command. I hoarded the treasure like a miser and made it last out the balance of my stay in Washington.

Our elderly colored cook, Liza, added greatly to the comfort of our Washington sojourn. Liza had come north from Georgia seeking employment shortly after the outbreak of the war when her only son had been drafted into the army. Her first job in Washington was in our home and she stayed with us until we returned to Chicago. She was always cheerful and willing, and an excellent cook as well.

When Liza first joined our household my wife advised her that I had one of the most important jobs in the government and that the best way for her to ensure the safe return of her son was to serve me my dinner whenever I might arrive home from work. The result was our evening meal took place anywhere from 7:30 to 9:30 at night.

Once my mother came on from Kansas City to pay us a visit for about a week. Being born and brought up on a plantation in Louisiana, she had fairly old fashioned ideas as to the handling of colored servants. On the morning of her departure, I was shaving in my bathroom and overheard a conversation in the kitchen between Mother and Liza. It went as follows:

Mother: "Liza, I am going back home to Kansas City today, and I am counting on you to take good care of my children. If I ever hear that you are not doing your job, I will make a special trip back to Washington just to pull every hair out of your head."

Liza: Yes'm, yes'm, I shore will—I shore will."

Of course, we had no air-conditioning at that time in Washington, either at home or in our offices. Anyone who has ever spent July and August in our nation's capital would never choose this spot as a summer resort. Although we certainly did not enjoy the intense muggy heat of the lower Potomac River, I cannot recall that it bothered us greatly. Perhaps this was partly the result of youth and partly because we had not yet been softened by the use of air-conditioning. Moreover, I was able to send my family for a month each summer to the eastern shore of Maryland where I joined them for my two-week vacations.

The intense work load at the War Production Board was alleviated for me by occasional brief visits to various military establishments in the eastern part of the United States. Of these I remember particularly a trip to the hills of central Pennsylvania where a small group of us witnessed the full-scale manoeuvres of an armored division. Also memorable was a visit to the Philadelphia Navy Yard where we made a complete tour of the battleship New Jersey, just then on the verge of being commissioned. The New Jersey, along with her sister ship, the Missouri, was the last and greatest of the battleships of World War II, and probably the last warship of its kind that will ever be built.

Docked right next to the New Jersey at the time was a British battleship that had come in for an overhaul. I cannot remember her name but I do recall that she was one of the main ships-of-the-line of Admiral Jellicoe's Grand Fleet of World War I. Compared to the sweeping lines and majestic size of the New Jersey, this British warship looked like a dumpy little tugboat.

Probably because I had little opportunity to attend official functions, I could never seem to get the hang of government protocol. Consequently, I found myself involved in a series of minor embarrassments. One of these occurred when my wife and I attended a dinner in Georgetown in honor of the ambassador from Jugoslavia. At eleven P.M., realizing that I had to be in my office at eight the next morning, I turned to my wife and said in a firm tone: "I think it is high time we started for home."

Immediately the ambassador sprang to his feet, grabbed his wife's hand, and announced that they had to leave at once.

On the way home my wife instructed me in no uncertain terms that, at a Washington dinner party, no one was supposed to leave until after the guest of honor had departed.

On another occasion I took a trip with Robert Patterson, the Undersecretary of War, and Fred Eberstadt to inspect an armored division at Camp Devon on Cape Cod just before its departure for Europe. We flew in the DC-3 that was assigned to the personal use of the Undersecretary.

155

When we landed at Camp Devon I happened to be seated right beside the exit at the rear. Without thinking, I led the procession down the steps of the plane. On emerging I found myself confronting a line of generals standing at attention. The first was the commanding officer of the division, a major-general. He was flanked on his left by two brigadier-generals.

The top brass looked somewhat startled and asked: "Are *you* Secretary Patterson?"

"Oh, no," said I airily, "Secretary Patterson is right behind me."

Some time later it was impressed upon me, quietly but firmly, that the top-ranking official is always the first to alight from whatever vehicle in which his party happens to be travelling.

An amusing incident occurred on this flight north to Camp Devon. As we flew over Connecticut we were suddenly buzzed by a P-39 fighter plane. This ship dove right under our tail and then ascended almost vertically not more than fifty feet in front of our nose. At this point I noticed Patterson scribbling on a pad the number of the plane. Ever since I have always regretted that I was not able to be present when the brash young pilot was confronted with the fact that he had buzzed the plane of the Undersecretary of War.

Perhaps it was the excitement of my work, and perhaps it was youth, but ever since I have looked back on my stay in Washington as one of the most interesting and stimulating periods of my life. Another important factor in this connection was the pleasure I had during these years in my children.

When they arrived in Washington my daughters, Alison and Anne, were ten and eight respectively, and my small son, Dickie, was four. All of them were still in the age of innocence, but in stages of development where a father could have the greatest enjoyment in being with them. Just prior to this time they had been infants, and almost immediately afterwards they began to depart for boarding schools.

My daughters were lovely girls, and it was wonderful to watch them grow in grace and understanding. My son, Dickie, however, was something a little different. He was a most ecstatic child, with no apparent inhibitions, and his excitement at every new experience that life offered—a trip to the zoo, a boat ride, or learning to swim—was always a joy to behold.

One Sunday evening in late 1942, Colonel and Mrs. J. Russell Forgan came to a family supper at our home. Russ Forgan and I have been partners in business since 1931 and we have been close friends since our college days at Princeton. At that time he was serving with the Army Service Forces in London, and had been sent back to Washington to expedite some badly needed supplies for the campaign in Africa. His wife, Ada, had come down from New York to be with him during his brief stay in this country.

After supper, while we were sitting in the living room, the three children came downstairs in their wrappers to say goodnight. After kissing his mother and father, Dickie took a long look at Ada Forgan, who was then, and still is, a very beautiful woman. All at once he made a flying dive for her lap to kiss her also. Unfortunately, Ada was wearing a hat and Dick found his cheek impaled on one of her hatpins. He backed away slowly rubbing his cheek. Then without crying or saying a word, he turned and went slowly upstairs.

The next morning at breakfast I said to him: "You know, Dickie, you will have to learn as you grow older that whenever you sniff at lovely roses you must always look out for the thorns."

In the summer of 1944 Dick learned to swim in the pool of the Chevy Chase Country Club. He was extremely vocal in his pride of accomplishment. Watching his antics with me one day was a near neighbor of ours, herself a mother of three small children. She suddenly turned to me and said: "I have come to the deliberate conclusion, John, that that son of yours is the world's most enchanting child."

It is memories such as these that I cling to ever since he was lost in an airplane disaster over the North Atlantic some fourteen years later.

Epilogue

T he job of allocating strategic materials during an all-out global war was not one designed to win a popularity contest. With an unlimited demand and severely limited supplies, it was not only impossible to please everybody, but it was not even possible to please anyone. Each claimant agency sent its representative to the table of the Requirements Committee thoroughly imbued with the conviction that only by obtaining the materials necessary to complete all of its own planned programs could the war be won. The chief trouble was that these convictions were, for the most part, completely sincere, no matter how myopic and biased they might appear to an objective observer.

159

When these representatives returned to their respective agencies they were always forced to report that they had been unable to obtain everything they had requested. Consequently, they found themselves subject to criticism by their superiors. The representatives in turn were bound to feel a sense of frustration and at least some resentment against the WPB officials whose decisions had placed them in this unhappy position.

I was thoroughly aware of this general attitude throughout my period of work with the Requirements Committee. Unfortunately, however, there was not very much I could do about it. Early in the game I realized that the best I could do was an attempt to convince everyone involved of my intellectual integrity, my sense of fairness, and my desire to do everything within the limits of my abilities to further the overall war effort. I can only hope that I succeeded in some measure in achieving these objectives.

Of course, as long as I occupied my official position, these feelings of resentment toward me were kept well under cover. It was interesting and even amusing, however, to notice how they came to the surface once my association with the War Production Board was terminated.

The pot boiled over on the evening of the farewell party given for me at the home of Maurice Wertheim. Attending this function were a large group of my associates from the WPB, as well as all the members of the Requirements Committee and of the Program Adjustment Committee. During the course of the evening I was the recipient of cracks of one kind or another from the representatives of most of the claimant agencies. These remarks were all made in a bantering fashion, doubtless aided by the releasing influence of alcohol, but beneath the surface it was easy to detect a note of seriousness. The most memorable comments, however, came at the end of the evening when everyone was saying goodbye.

First came General Hopkins of the Air Force, who addressed me as follows: "I must tell you, John, that your greatest contribution to the war effort is your current resignation from the War Production Board."

Next came Captain Small of the Navy. While shaking my hand he said: "You will never realize, John, the hours I have spent pacing the floor at night, trying to figure out how I could get around that bastard, Fennelly."

The finest compliment of all was reserved for the last. It came from a former associate of mine on the WPB staff, Dr. Melvin de Chazeau. His statement was: "You know, John, I really hate to see you leave because you are the most successful son of a bitch I have ever seen in action."

Appendix

*The viewpoint
of a
non-interventionist*

December 4, 1940

Herbert Agar, Esq.,
The Courier-Journal
Louisville, Kentucky

Dear Herbert:

I read with great interest the other day your editorial entitled "The Lotus Eaters". Just one year ago, when you and I last exchanged ideas, we were completely agreed that the greatest disaster which could befall this country would be to become involved in the European conflict, and that every intelligent American should be constantly on his guard against the strong pull ot emotionalism and propaganda which might lead us down the road to war. From your editorial, it is clear that your views have changed to a point where now you believe our only salvation lies in an immediate and wholehearted participation in the struggle on the side of Britain against the menace of Hitlerism. I, on the other hand, still feel exactly as we both felt one year ago.

162

The atmosphere is already so charged with emotion that it is exceedingly difficult to discuss this matter in a calm and dispassionate manner. Anyone who is not completely in sympathy with the idea of throwing our entire weight into the scales against Germany is written down as a Nazi, a Fifth Columnist, an appeaser, and even a Lotus Eater. In place of such nonsensical name calling, I should like to appeal to you as one intellectually honest American to another, in an effort to clarify my earnest groping for the truth which apparently seems so crystal-clear to you.

The time is fully ripe for such a discussion. We are already at the eleventh hour of decision in this matter, and that awful decision, when it is made, will have consequences which will reach not only into every corner of the globe but also far into the lives of our children and grandchildren. There is nothing so important to think about today. The saving grace, from my standpoint, is that the final decision yet lies before us; there is still a choice to be made. Although we are a long way down the road, we are not yet actually at war, and we still have, in my opinion, a few fleeting moments in which to face this tremendous issue squarely.

At the outset, I wish to say that I am completely in accord with your view that our present anomalous policy of giving 'all aid to Britain short of war' is immoral in several of its aspects and consequences. It is immoral because it is leading us steadily toward war while lulling the great majority of the American people into the belief that it is the only way in which we can avoid war. It is immoral because many who advocate it most strenuously do not believe what they are saying. They really believe secretly, as you believe forthrightly, that we should declare war on Germany, but they feel that the American public is not yet ready to accept such an unpalatable decision, and must be led with blinders on, like a horse out of a burning stable. It is immoral because it asks another nation to do our fighting for us. Either this is our war, or it is not. If I thought it were, I should feel, like you, a sense of shame in permitting the British people to bear the full brunt of the holocaust while we sit back and give them only such aid as they can pay for with cash. If it is not our war, on the other hand, it is obvious that we should have no part of it, except to promote the earliest possible return of peace.

Finally, this attitude is immoral because it tends to raise false hopes in the minds of the British people. We are, of course, doing exactly the same sort of thing to the Chinese people. Both of

163

these nations today are confident that, if they can hang on a little while longer, they will have the entire weight of our tremendous economic and human resources supporting them in their struggles. You and I know that Great Britain cannot hope to win a cleancut victory in this war by her own efforts alone, and it is improbable that she can even hope to win as a result of our present aid and that which is still on order. It is thus entirely possible that if the British knew now that our support is to be limited by the amount of their cash resources, they might think it wise to seek an early peace on some kind of a compromise basis. I strongly suspect that the same situation applies in the case of China. We have, therefore, a strong moral obligation to the British and Chinese people as well as to ourselves to clarify this issue as quickly as possible. Otherwise, our aid may be merely the cause of prolonging the struggle, and in that case we must assume a large measure of responsibility for the needless slaughter of many British and Chinese citizens.

We can agree then that the issue is fairly simple and clear. Either we cast the die and enter the war with all our strength and fight wholeheartedly until the Germans (and Japanese) are crushed, or else we stay out and make it abundantly clear to the British and Chinese that we have no intention of coming in. You would pursue the former course forthrightly, while I should follow the latter. I believe that one should only choose a deliberate path to war if one's vision as to the costs and consequences is clear and certain. If one is a man of good will, he must have the courage of burning convictions to elect a course which can only bring widespread death and destruction in its wake.

I think you believe, and I agree, that unless we throw our whole weight behind Britain, we shall probably face at the best a compromise peace or stalemate, and at the worst, a complete German victory. Let us then assume the worst; a victory for Hitler within the next few months, involving a surrender of the British fleet. I should be more than foolish if I did not admit that such a situation would create more peril for the United States than that which exists today. I do believe, however, that our position would be very far from desperate. We have both heard all the arguments pro and con on this subject, and I am sure I do not need to go into them here. Suffice it to say that I feel totally unafraid, on what to me are convincing grounds, to face this eventuality. Our geographical immunity, our overwhelming economic

164

resources, the exhausted and starved condition of Europe, and the necessity which Germany will face of subduing and organizing her conquered victims all combine to convince me that this country has an assured immunity from actual attack for at least several years, unless we force such an attack by our own intemperate actions. If we do not employ this breathing spell to build our defenses to a point where we can withstand any possible attack, we shall not deserve to be saved.

Yes, I know that old argument about being isolated in a hostile world of totalitarianism. As a student of American history, you realize, of course, that we have been relatively isolated throughout most of our national history. You know that, during the first half century of this republic, we were a solitary and struggling democracy in a hostile world of kings, emperors and dictators. We survived then, and we shall survive much more easily today. I wonder if it has occurred to you that, if we shall be isolated from Europe, Europe will likewise be isolated from America, and it is my conviction that Europe is more dependent upon America than America upon Europe.

The point is I cannot be frightened by these spectres, and I am sure that many millions of Americans feel likewise, but most of them now are brow-beaten into silence by the dislike of being thought pro-Nazi. Furthermore, I do not believe that the American people will ever elect consciously to go to war as a result of this campaign of fear. If they do go in, it will be because they have been led over the brink by subterfuge, and I am sure that you, of all people, would never condone such tactics. I remember sitting up with you most of a night, many years ago, while you set forth your philosophic conviction that no end, however, laudable, could ever justify dishonest means, and certainly you will agree that it is dishonest to lead this country to war while promising to keep it out.

The fact is, Herbert, I cannot believe that you yourself are afraid of the prospect of an actual attack on this country. I am convinced that you, and many like you, are burning with a passion to lead a crusade against the powers of darkness, and in the complex of your emotions fear does not enter. Yet you bemean yourselves by preaching your crusade to the American people almost solely in terms of fear. You do us an injustice, because we are just as capable as you of waging war in a holy cause if we can be convinced that the cause is holy. In fact it is the only kind of

165

war we are willing to wage. We shall never follow your crusade if your only appeal is to our sense of fear.

We entered the last European War, not because of fear, but because we believed we had a holy cause to make the world safe for democracy. We know now we did not succeed in this attempt, and we have been somewhat disillusioned ever since about that kind of a crusade. What is our holy cause today? Is it to save democracy? If it is just that, many of us are fearful that we shall lose democracy in the United States while trying to rescue it for Europe and become Nazis as a result of our efforts to crush Nazism.

Do you really think it is possible for us, together with Britain, to reconquer the continent to Europe from the Germans without tremendous efforts and sacrifices over many years of warfare? If you believe us capable of this achievement, you surely cannot believe, at the same time, that our country is in danger of being overrun by the Germans. I am sure you must agree there can be no genuine victory over Germany unless her armies are crushed in battle on the soil of Europe. Are you prepared to face the full implications of such an undertaking?

Let us suppose for a moment that such an outcome is possible. Do you think that we are capable of organizing a permanent and just peace in Europe, and have you a blueprint of the new political and social order which we shall create? You cannot believe that the status quo ante bellum will automatically reappear after the defeat of Germany. I, for one, am certain I should never be willing to wage a crusade for the restoration of a status quo which was the primary cause of the present troubles. How can we hope to create a United States of Europe by means of pressure from without, and how can this be achieved in any event without leaving Germany in a dominant position? The only answer I can see to this is to kill off some eighty million Germans, an undertaking I should not relish. Is it not possible that the net result of all our efforts would be to create greater chaos and injustice than exists today?

Do you feel Britain can be expected to organize a permanent peace in Europe? You know, perhaps better than I, that never in her entire history has she taken a constructive attitude toward the European Continent. Instead her main interest has been the negative one of thwarting the rise of any single power to a position of predominance. Even granting a change of heart in this connection, I am convinced that Britain will be physically as incapable of providing leadership for Europe after the end of this war as France was after the end of the last war.

As a student of economics I have believed for many years that Britain, as a leading world power, has become an economic anachronism. The British Empire was built up by sea power and water borne trade, and before the development of internal transportation made possible the rise of great continental empires, such as the United States and Russia. The growth of mass production technology in this country has swept on past England and left her with an industrial plant which is now archaic and largely obsolete. Her 'tight little isle' and overseas possessions do not give her sufficient market scope to develop mass production methods and she is falling behind steadily in the competitive struggle. Political power is inseparable from economic power, and I can only believe that Britain's star is on the wane in both respects. If this be true, shall we be wise in the long run if we make a bet on Britain's ability to restore and maintain a permanent peace in Europe?

Is it not possible that the most intelligent and moral role for the United States would be to work actively for an early peace both in Europe and in Asia? Instead of promoting peace today, we are merely promoting a continuation of war on both continents. In fact, we are playing the same kind of negative power politics which we condemn so heartily in the case of other nations. Why can we not assume a positive and constructive leadership for peace? We might say to Britain that we are willing to support her to the utmost in an effort to obtain an early peace which would preserve her freedom and leave her navy and overseas empire intact. At the same time, we should inform her that, if she is determined to fight on until Germany is crushed, she will have to fight alone.

We are today in a tremendously powerful strategic position to use our influence for peace if we choose to do so. It is clear to me that Britain will not continue much longer the conflict without our full support, and that Germany would greatly prefer an inconclusive peace to our wholehearted entrance into the struggle against her. Unless they destroy one another utterly, Britain and Germany must find a way of living together in Europe, and they can probably find it as well today as they can five years hence.

Most Americans love and admire the British people as much as they dislike Hitler and his followers. All our sentiments and emotions pull us toward the British and away from the Germans, but this is not enough. It is easy to win our hearts for your crusade—you have them already—but you must also win our heads. And this you have not done.

Very sincerely yours,
JOHN F. FENNELLY